THE QUEST

A Search for the Grail
of
Immortality

BY THE SAME AUTHOR

The Way — Part Two of the Quest Series
Welsh/Celtic Nature Magic
The Thirteen Treasures
The Sword of Dyrnwyn
Healing through the Use of Celtic Crystal Magick
Psychometry and Psychic Development
Welsh/Celtic Festivals
Celtic Meditation Techniques
Sexual Energy
Welsh/Celtic Folklore
The Wisdom of the Cymmry

THE QUEST

A Search for the Grail of Immortality

by

RHUDDLWM GAWR
and
MARCY EDWARDS

Illustrations by Craig Hamilton and Bill Wheeler

CAMELOT PRESS
Athens, Georgia

First published in the United States of America 1980
Second Edition Hardcover, 250 Registered Copies 1985
Reprinted Paperback 1985

Camelot Press Ltd.
P.O. Box 4196
Athens, Georgia 30605

ISBN 0-931760-01-1
Library of Congress Catalog Number 78-61716

Manufactured in the United States of America for the Publisher by
COPPLE HOUSE BOOKS, INC.
Lakemont, Georgia 30525

ACKNOWLEDGMENTS

In 1972 this book was only a germ in the mind of its author, Rhuddlwm Gawr. In the ten years since its inception, the book has been refined, researched, argued about, and generally rewritten several dozen times.

Two of us collaborated on this book; Rhuddlwm Gawr, providing inspiration and text, and Marcy Edwards, rewriting and editing.

The many other people who helped, include:

Brian Garrette, who added literary criticism much appreciated; Charon Moga and Kathy Cagle who originally typed the first few chapters; Sirce, who added needed feminist thoughts concerning non-sexism; Bobbie Willis, who offered constructive criticism; Selena Fox, who encouraged and corrected English usage; Terri Kay, who typed the final draft; and Mary Sue, a wife who understood.

For us the preparation of this book has itself been a Quest. It has been permeated with spiritual purpose and Joy.

Come--Join the dance.

Rhuddlwm Gawr

CONTENTS

ILLUSTRATIONS

THE QUEST
Introduction

This book is about enlightenment--It also reveals the
truth about Dinwn Mwyn   and   the Ancient Religion of Wales--
Dewianath Cymmry.

You can't learn about the old religion from reading a
book. You learn from experiencing the cycle of nature, for
the Old Religion is one of life and joy; relinking one's self
and others with nature. It is a reawakening of the primal
energies which once flowed through the veins of human-kind.
It is the feeling of joy when a robin lights on the branch of
a young tree and sings the song of Spring. It is the wonder
in a child's eye when she witnesses the birth of a puppy for
the first time. It is seeing Autumn leaves drift downward
from beautifully painted trees. It is lying in a fragrant
Summer meadow and watching the clouds form into wonderfully
varied shapes and it is found in a shaded alcove of a garden
where a statue of the Goddess rests.

This book describes a particular tradition of Dewianath Cymmry
and although primarily for those who already have some knowledge of the Old Religion, those readers who either know
nothing of the craft or, worse, have a complete misconception
of the subject, are not ignored.

The story of Dewianath Cymmry is as old as the human
race and goes back to the beginning of human consciousness
when the first primitive conception of the existence of outside forces was personalized in the concept of a duality.
These two deities, one male and one female, are found in the
pantheon of all religions. They are the personification of
the balance of opposites: light and darkness; summer and
winter; life and death; sowing and harvest; male and female.

1

Dewianath Cymmry has a direct link with the ancient religion
of Atlantis, an ancient civilization which legend reports existed
on a great island to the west of Europe. Over ten thousand
years ago, a horrible cataclysm caused this island to sink
into the ocean, leaving its survivors to make for the nearest
land. Some chose the Americas, some went to Africa, and some
sailed to northern Europe. They all carried the same occult
heritage with them which influenced every civilization they
touched upon. Unfortunately, most of this knowledge has since
either been lost completely or overlaid by other religions
so that it is but a shadow of what it once was.

But, in Wales, and elsewhere, the "hidden people" and
their brothers and sisters still worship the old deities and
patiently wait the coming of the New Age when they may again
reveal the undefiled "sacred knowlege" to the world.

Wales is a broad indented peninsula lying in the south-
western part of Great Britain and divided into thirteen
countries. Each country is divided into smaller portions,
cantrefs, and a myriad of postal districts and religious
parishes. Racially, the Welsh are of Celtic stock, lithe
and handsome. The pride and spirit of the Welsh stems from
their Celtic warrior heritage.

Their grand mountains and hauntingly beautiful valleys
have inspired poetry and song for well over two thousand
years. Even today, the Welsh still cling to their own outlook
and spirit, and many still use their own language, older than
the English Nation of which they are a part.

It is within this small "country-within-a-country" that
we discover the origins of the Authurian Romances, the hidden
spiritual strength of Great Britain, and one of the last
bastions of the ancient Atlantean mysteries.

In revealing these mysteries, this book also tells the
story of Rhuddlwm Gawr and his quest for the Magickal Grail
of Immortality.

CHAPTER ONE

The Birth of a Seeker

3

CHAPTER ONE

THE BEGINNING

"The path is one for all, the means to reach the
Goal must vary with the pilgrim." -H. P. Blavatsky

The month after I graduated from high school, two friends
of mine, Lonny and Bob, invited me to go mountain climbing in
Canada. I had had considerable experience the previous two
summers in the Appalachians and had really enjoyed myself, so
I readily agreed. We left our home in Orlando, Florida by
bus on the twenty-third of July and arrived in Calgary,
British Columbia on the thirtieth.

From the start, things just seemed to fall apart. First,
some of our climbing gear was lost in transit and we had to
rent expensive and unfamiliar equipment. Then we were delayed
three full days while Lonny got over a case of dysentery.
When we finally began, things went from bad to worse. On the
way to the jumping off point, our rental Jeep broke down one
mile from our destination and we had to walk the rest of the
way. Then, when we finally began climbing, we hadn't gone
fifty meters, when I dropped half the rations down the face
of the cliff and had to rapel down to pick them up. Shortly
afterwards, Bob dropped his pick down a crevice. That
incident took twenty minutes to correct. We had certainly made
an "inauspicious" beginning.

We made several quick runs from ledge to ledge until we
were halfway up the face of the mountain. Then, while Bob and
Lonny rested, I surveyed the remainder of the climb. It was
going to be rougher than we thought, and I was beginning to
have lousy feelings about the whole thing. I realized, however,
that it was going to be just as easy to climb the rest of the

4

way as to go back down at this point.

I rapelled back down to Bob and Lonny. "It's going to be hell, Lonny, but I'm game. How about you, Bob?"

Bob was visibly fatigued. "I guess so," he moaned.

I was lead climber. After five moves up I paused to study the holds that would take us over the rougher section ahead. They were small but solid. It was looking better now. Standing on the tips of my toes, I turned my right foot out and lifted it to a fissure that I had seen from below. I transferred my weight to my right foot and it felt solid. I jammed my right hand into another crack and pulled. My movements were feeling natural and sensuous. I was moving faster now, with more confidence and this gave me a joyous feeling. Maybe I got a little careless. I was moving my left foot from one hold to another when something seemed to break free or maybe I just slipped.

A strange thing happened then. It seemed as though everything congealed and froze. That is the only way I can describe it. I was floating! Things around me were moving very, very slowly and as I turned, I saw a body not ten feet away drifting slowly, slowly toward the cliff wall. As the face came into view, I saw that it was me! I seemed to be outside my body, floating and watching myself slam into the side of a mountain in slow motion!

It is a strange and frightening feeling, looking at yourself, and many thoughts ran through my mind. I can't remember very much of it today, except some brief flashes--I was thinking about my lousy grades in English, and my Mom, and I have a hazy recollection of some religious feeling.

Then I became aware of a presence nearby, and as I slowly, slowly turned, I saw her!

It was the face of the most beautiful woman I had ever seen. But all I could see was her face. The rest of her was misty. She wore a concerned, somewhat curious, expression.

"Please re-enter your body, William. It's not time yet for you to pass on, for there is much remaining for you to do.

5

Relax and let me help."

I suddenly felt an overpowering tension which drew me
back to my body. The next thing I knew, it snapped and I was
hanging upside down by the safety line about forty feet below
Bob. Things were moving normally again, and I became aware
of his frantic shouts.

"Are you all right? Jesus Christ, Bill!! Shit, Bill!!
Are you OK?"

"Yeah! Help me get out of here!"

"Just hang on. We'll be right down."

I spent some time in the emergency room of the Calgary
hospital, but they could find nothing seriously wrong except
a slight concussion. I didn't say anything about the out-of-
body experience. I didn't quite know what to say. I was
frightened by it, but also somewhat awed and perplexed.
I thought it was just an hallucination caused by the head
injury; but it was so real!

Little did I know that seven years later, again while
climbing a mountain, I was to meet the lady of my vision,
and this time she would have a body!

* * * *

It was the Spring of 1965. I had gotten my fondest wish.
Ever since my tour of duty with the Marine Corps I had wanted
to take a trip to Europe. But one thing and then another had
come up. I went from job to job but always worked in the
States or in the Carribean. Now my dream was coming true.

I had been sent to the Island of Majorca as a Civilian
electronics instructor on an Airforce contract. It was supposed to be hardship duty, but considering the fact that the
base was located ten miles from a beautiful Mediterranean
resort, I began to have doubts about the accuracy of that
part of the pre-mission briefing within ten minutes after I
landed!

Majorca has been called the " Golden Island" because of
the haze which seems to hover above it. Much of the country
is orchard land, with olive, fig and almond trees. Wildflowers

6

grow everywhere. It is an amazingly beautiful place,
especially in the Springtime. I couldn't believe my good
luck in pulling this sort of "hardship duty."

The first week I explored the beaches, bars and clubs,
happily gliding along on the carefree pace, enjoying the pretty
girls and gaiety of night life. But soon I was restless again;
the soaring cliffs above the sea goaded me. I wandered upward
beyond the coastal villages, seeking simple pleasure and peace
in the sweetness of spring--the wildflowers on the hillsides
were everywhere and the orchards of lemons, oranges, and almonds were fresh with blossoms. The terrace slopes were
beautiful ascending from the glittering sea. Puig Major, the
highest mountain, was the name mentioned by various residents
as a worthy match for an adventurous climber. And with determination, I set aside a few days in June to attempt the climb.
The dramatic north face was tempting, but the precipitous
three-thousand foot drop to the sea was a bit insane considering the climb was to be solo. I decided to climb the
easier south side.

It went fantastically! The sun was lighting the sea as
I started off and the scenery was breathtaking. I don't
believe there are words to describe what it felt like climbing that mountain. I was part of it! My hands and feet seemed
to flow over the rocks. The breeze was fresh and exhilarating
and I felt as though I could have soared into it like an eagle.
My body had a rhythm of its own which felt like the heartbeat
of the mountain. This was the best climb of my life.

I was still exhilarated from the experience when I
scrambled over one edge of the small plateau at the summit,
got to my feet and immediately began wandering around, breathing deeply but regularly, looking everywhere at the wonderful
view.

At first she was unrecognizable as a woman. She might
have been a rock or a brown hillock. Then, as I came closer,
I saw two sets of bare toes half hidden, but half revealed

under a sort of great cloak which covered the rest of the
body completely. I was a little irritated at this invasion
of my anticipated solitude, but there was no point in trying
to recapture my feelings of the last few minutes. I was
going to walk over and say hello, which I suppose was the
natural thing to do, when something stopped me. Maybe it
was the absolute stillness--a motionless body, arms apparently
clasped around legs and forehead to knees, covered by a cloak
that the breezes scarcely seemed to touch. I stopped and sat
down a few feet directly in front of the feet. I had only to
wait a few minutes before the figure stirred.

She threw the hood of the cloak or cape back with a toss
of her head and stared straight at me. In the instant before
I realized it was her, I thought she looked disoriented and
vacant. Then, instantly I flashed back to that August day in
Canada. The same eyes! The same dark hair! The same beautiful face! I went clammy! Something hit me in the stomach.
I must have looked as if I were going to pass out--and maybe
I would have--because her brow furrowed and the same concerned
look I remembered passed across her face.

"Are you all right?" she asked. Her voice had a beautiful tone, throaty and musical, with a British accent.

"Who are you?" I stammered.

She arched her eyebrows, "Sarah."

"Why have you come back to me?"

She looked at me, calmly, inviting my stammerings and
questions, then said quietly, "I don't think I understand."

"I mean. . ." I was stunned. The exact same face! No
sign of age, the same hairstyle, the same woman!

"I'm afraid you have me confused with someone else,"
she said in an amused tone. It was obvious she thought I was
trying to pick her up. "I'm sorry, but if you're all right
now, I have to be getting back to the hotel."

"Wait!" I cried. "It's just that. . . Oh damn! You'll
never believe me," I cried miserably.

8

The path down puig major

She cocked her head to one side. "All right. I guess I have a few minutes. Go ahead, tell me."

I told her. It was hard because I had never told anyone before, but not that hard, because it was her and she listened attentively.

"You say that you felt as though you were out of your body, and you saw my face?" she asked.

I saw that she had a strange expression on her face and I misunderstood. "Oh, I knew you wouldn't believe me, but the coincidence was just too fantastic, I had to tell you."

"On the contrary," she said quietly. "I do believe you." She got to her feet. For the first time she noticed my clothes. "Did you climb up here?" she asked increduously.

"Yeah, I came up the south side. How did you get here?"

"There is a path down the east slope."

As we walked down the steep pathway I wondered about her. "What were you doing up there?" I asked.

"I'm afraid I can't discuss that," was her reply. After a minute or two of awkward silence I asked her where she was staying and whether I could see her again. Instead of answering, she stopped and looked straight into my eyes.

"If you meet me on the dock in front of the excursion boat tomorrow at three o'clock, I will take you on a journey from which you will never return."

With a puzzled expression on my face, I blurted "Huh? What does that mean?"

"You'll have to meet me there to find out," she smiled. "That is, if you want to."

She said goodbye, waved, and was gone.

I was staying in a rented room in the hotel manager's house, since I didn't have a reservation for the latter half of June, and there weren't adequate facilities at the Air Force base. It was a mud-plastered little apartment which was more of a basement than anything else, with a large boulder protruding from one corner. The manager said that when they built the house they couldn't move the damn thing so they just

10

left it. I thought it gave the room a rustic look. Besides, it was a great conversation piece in my quest for female companionship. "Want to come over to my apartment and see my rock?" I would ask.

"Your what?" she would answer. One thing would lead to another and I would con another bird into my lair.

Of course, I met her at the dock the next day. And the next, and the next. In fact I saw her every chance I could, but since I was working on a government contract for the Air Force, my hours didn't always match her schedule. I knew it wasn't love or sex fascination, but there was an attraction I couldn't define.

The first day on the boat, just as we were chugging away, Sarah asked, "Are you a religious person, William?"

"Yes, I guess so," I answered.

"Well, what do you believe in? I mean really. Do you believe in a God and Jesus Christ? Do you believe in heaven and angels?"

I was looking at her body and thinking about the rock in my apartment. "Hell, Sarah, I don't know. I guess I've never really thought about it." I was a little annoyed about the subject she was choosing for discussion. "I grew to be very involved in church work, back home, but the last few years haven't given me much of an opportunity to really think about what I believe in and I don't usually talk about it much."

She had the bluest eyes that I had ever seen and they seemed to swallow me up.

"William, what is your birthday?" she asked, her eyes wide.

"June the twenty-first."

She seemed to stiffen and her breathing quickened. There was no longer anything casual about the questions.

"Nineteen-forty. Why?"

She ignored that and asked several questions relating to my parents and my ancestry.

11

The Library

12

"Well, my father and mother were divorced when I was about a year old. My father was English and American Indian and my mother was German and Irish." I guess I was ignorant of my ancestry but I told her all I could remember. "I was raised in the United States by my grandmother who was a Bible-quoting Southern Baptist. No one in the family talked much about their history. Their interests were directed toward the impending Second Coming."

I was curious as to the reason for her continuous questions, but I couldn't seem to get her to give me a straight answer. Nor would she talk about herself beyond where she was from.

For several days we spoke of philosophy and religion and fairy tales. We argued about whether there was a soul and we discussed the meaning of reincarnation. She was a fantastic storehouse of knowledge and could apparently converse intelligently on any subject.

I soon realized that my normal thought of sex and conquest were curiously absent. In fact I was a little annoyed at not being my usual macho self.

We were lying on a lonely stretch of beach at the mouth of the harbour one afternoon, basking in the sun, not saying much when she asked me, "William?"

"Hmmm?" I murmured. I felt lazy and content and warm.

"When are you going to make love to me?"

My eyes snapped open so fast I almost rolled them up into my head and I sat bolt upright. "Huh? What the hell kind of question is that?" I blurted out. "I mean, shit, Sarah."

"There is no need to use profanity," she calmly said.

"Well, of course, Duchess. Anything you say." There was sarcasm in my voice as I tried to hide my utter confusion. "Shit."

"Well?" she murmured.

"Well, what?" I said tightly.

"When-are-you-going-to-make-love-to-me?"

13

I looked deeply and questioningly into her eyes, and suddenly all the lines of bullshit, all the tricks I had used before became as nothing. I took her hand in mine as I arose and pulled her up. We put our arms around each other and slowly walked back to my room.

For the first time in my life there was no rush. Also, for the first time in my life I discovered what the phrase "making love" really meant.

And later, after we made love, as we lay side by side in the gathering dusk, arms around each other, I finally began to get answers to some of the many questions I had asked.

"William, when you described your Canadian vision and out-of-body experience the day we first met, I knew that I was destined to be your guide. I also knew that you were a special person and blessed by the Goddess." She rolled over and peered into my face. "I also knew you were a male chauvinist son of a bitch."

"What?" I exclaimed. "You can't mean that! Didn't I treat you with respect and consideration?"

"Oh yes, with about as much consideration as a Sherman tank!" she replied.

I thought for a while. "Oh, I guess you have a point. I did come on strong at times."

"William, you were an egotistical bastard when I first met you. You still are, but you're beginning to show promise."

"Just what do you mean by that?" I snapped.

"I mean that I have watched a typical male chauvinist, with male animal hangups start to become a human person with honest feelings." My head started to swell. "But, who still needs to work out his ego problems." She placed a quick, pecking kiss on my lips, grinned, then kissed me again, much more slowly this time.

The days flew by. Too soon it was time for her to return to London from her holiday. The day she was leaving I awoke to her soft fingers stroking the skin of my shoulder. I pulled her over on top of me and wrapped my legs around hers. "I don't want you to leave, Sarah," I said.

14

"I know," she said with a hint of moisture in her eyes.
"But the time has come. I can only promise this: When you
wish to learn more about me and my way, come to me. I'll be
waiting."

She gave me her address, which I placed in my suitcase,
and vowed I would never lose it. Two weeks later she was a
memory which tugged at my insides when I thought of her.
A month later, I was shacked up with a Greek-American high
school teacher from Pennsylvania.

But over the next few months in my travels from Madrid
to Athens to Rome and finally to Venice I thought about her
more and more often, and I thought about our conversations.

When I first knew I had to see her again, I was already
in London and tired and hungry. I was on my way back to the
States on a leave of absence. I had been in Europe long
enough. I wanted to see a modern bathroom again, and I
wanted to hear familiar voices.

"Hell, I should call her, but it's been months. I wonder
if she really wants to see me again. I didn't even write."
I thought I would surprise her so I had the taxi stop a block
away and I walked the rest of the way.

She had a flat in the rear of a brownstone house on the
second floor. There was no way she could have known I was
coming, but when I knocked on the door her voice called out,
"Come in, William. I'm in the kitchen." She knew I was
coming! Yet she couldn't have! When I asked her how she
knew, she only commented on how tired I looked and told me
dinner would be ready by the time I had a bath.

Later, over tea, she finally answered my questions. She
called herself a "Gwiddon"--a Welsh Witch, she translated.
I wouldn't have known a Witch from a helicopter! She was
twenty-three, unmarried and a priestess of the fifth level.
We sat up for hours with Sarah doing most of the talking,
before we fell into bed--too exhausted, too drained, to think
of sex.

15

The next day we left together for Wales. I didn't even call to terminate my contract. Sarah had to return to London almost at once, but I stayed on in a small village in northern Wales. At times I thought of her and at times I thought of home, but, I stayed--partly because she said I had to, partly because of the challenge, but mostly because I was learning.

I learned of the Cauldron of Cerridwen, and I found the Thirteen Treasures of Y Tylwyth Teg.

The Elder was speaking:

"William, before you embark upon this journey, know that once you have begun, there can be no turning back. For, if after we accept you, you should leave this place before the end of your instruction, your mind shall destroy itself."

With Sarah gone I felt alone, shaky, but still curiously excited.

They stood facing me, nine of them. If anyone had walked in upon that strange confrontation at that moment, they would have thought very little of it. They were dressed as ordinary Welsh men and women, farmers and storekeepers. I was the only one in a robe.

"William, have you read the twelve keys and comprehended their meaning?"

"Yes," I stammered.

"Then, know ye all present that William, a seeker, having read and comprehended the twelve keys, wishes to submit himself to the mystery of the first level and undergo the ordeal. He offers himself as a candidate and as a receptacle."

Thus began my instruction.

* * * * *

We arose at dawn each day, took a ritual bath and then filed out to the fields where we worked for an hour before breakfast. I thought I had worked hard before in my life. I hadn't even begun to exercise my muscles! There were weeds to pull, there were rows to hoe, and there were animals to feed.

Upon returning to the main building, we took another
ritual bath and partook of the morning meal. Although there
was no meat with the meal, it provided more than enough
sustenance.   There were eggs, soup, bread, vegetables, and
goats milk.

As each of us completed our meal, we went to the altar
room for morning meditation. We were taught the Cymmry method
of meditation, which was to lie down flat on the wooden floor
with feet about a foot apart and hands away from the body.
Then certain mental processes were formed. I was told that
this method, used to quiet the mind and activate the psychic
centers, was over twenty thousand years old! It seemed a
simple enough procedure at first, but it was almost a month
before I felt the changes that told me I had mastered it.
After an hour of meditation we again trudged out to the fields
where we laboured until about ten o'clock. We then came back
to our rooms to bathe again before our first lessons of the
day.

"We are the guardians of the thirteen Books of Y Tylwyth
Teg, the thirteen sacred treasures of the Welsh, in which are
to be found the secret knowledge of the ancients," related our
history guide. "In our religion, we worship the Great Spirit
in the forms of the God and Goddess. We do not promise anything, but, if the seeker looks hard enough at the truths we
offer, he or she will find love, knowledge and power. We
turn away none who wish to learn more of the wisdom of the
Cymmry. Our only requirement is that the seeker complete
the instructions, go on his or her quest, and be named before
he or she is allowed to be "adopted" into the clan of the
"Gentle Folk." We teach the way to enlightenment, and along
that pathway you will learn the magick of Nature."

As the Guide paused, my mind wandered. I was already
beginning to be touched by the magick of the early morning
light through the mist of the mountain valleys; the craggy
plateau, the rolling uplands, the old stone houses half-hidden

17

in the brush and berries. The ancient place had begun to grow
vine-like along the old stone walls of my consciousness,
softening the shadows.

The Guide continued.

"The thirteen treasures of the Cymmry are symbols of
the knowledge brought to Wales by the Ancient Ones. These
are the most important of our symbols after the Sacred Triads.

"While the Triads are direct representations of the Great
Spirit--the God/Goddess, the thirteen treasures are representative of the direct effects that the universe has upon the
souls of men and women, and thirteen is the symbol of the
thirteen lunar months.

"Each treasure has several meanings--an astrological one,
a mythological one, and a mystical one--all symbolic of our
philosophy. The thirteen treasures are also our Thirteen Books
of Knowledge. We, of the tribe of Gentle Folk, have traditionally withheld our secrets from the common people, because of
their inability to understand. But, for those who seek us,
we can be found. We have attracted people from all religions,
where they have found perfect unity, peace, and mutual dedication to the truth.

"Our philosophy exceeds history's finest religions and
appeals logically to the critical seeker. You who have hungered for those deep answers which you have been unable to
find thus far, have now opened your mind to truth, casting
out those entrenched prejudices which have caused you confusion and anguish. You who have now joined us, and proven
worthy, characteristically possess that rare trait of maturity
only found in the best minds.

"When a person is joyful, loving and confident, he or
she is naturally attuned to the Great Spirit of Love. When a
person is fearful, hateful and without hope, he or she is
attuned to the evil forces of fear, hate and despair. Humankind alone is responsible for evil, for it is within your
own nature to make a choice. You can rise up from evil by

learning truth and putting it into everyday practice, or you can fall into the mire of deception. One day your knowledge of truth will gain you freedom from the evil of the world."

A great deal of reading was required in connection with the instructions. When I was taken to the library, seemingly a small building set against one side of the hill, I was totally unprepared for the sheer size of the place. I assumed there would be a small room with a few books, but the visible building was just the entrance. I never did explore the entire complex because of restrictions but there must have been dozens of corridors and an uncountable number of rooms. The library was situated in the southern section of the hill and contained several thousand volumes, which, according to the historian, were all that were left when the ancient library on the isle of Anglesley was burned by the Romans.

*　*　*　*　*

The lunch bell would ring at midday, with a meal of eggs, vegetables, dark bread, and mead. We then retired for one hour of private meditation before returning to the fields.

I had never worked so hard in my life as I did in those fields! My muscles and even my bones ached terribly. After two hours of bone wrenching, back breaking labor, we were allowed to return to our rooms where we bathed, and, after an hour's rest, meditated alone until it was time for dinner. After the meal, we took part in the general cleanup of the meeting place and our own rooms.

Each day at sundown we were led to a slight rise to the west of the village where we performed the "rite of the praising of the Sun." We were told to concentrate on actually bringing the essence of the sun's energy into our bodies. This was to be done by sitting with our legs crossed and facing the sun with our eyes closed. We then imagined the Golden Light of the sun pouring into our bodies like a river.

At first it was an intellectual exercise but then I began to relax and melt into the dusk, my fatigue overcoming me. I thought I would sleep and let the mountains near the

19

village wall off all further learning, but the sunlight
always found a craggy hole to pass through and the light
bathed my face and poured into my body.

These alternate periods of hard physical work, meditation
and study created passages in my being I had never experienced
before. I began to sense a new labyrinth of feeling and
understanding. And so, just as I began to float beautifully
in the warm energetic sensations of sunset, I was pulled back
to a different level of conscious reality with the practice
of breathing and gymnastic exercise. I would breathe in to
the count of nine and breathe out to the count of seven, in
a regular rhythm. Later I was to learn that this is very
similar to yoga pranayama, which accomplishes the dual task
of relaxing the mind and making it more alert by forcing more
oxygen into the bloodstream.

A state of euphoria eased off again as we were stretched
painfully into a period of physical exercises, with strenuous
pulling at the soft bends of our muscles. Two hours of tor-
tuous exertion, then we were dismissed and we staggered to
our rooms where we took our final ritual bath of the day.

It was close to eleven p.m.; evening lessons were just
beginning. Our history guide was speaking: a distant chant
into my mind that was already numb and saturated. Then a
quiet watchfulness prevailed.

"Hear this, O lowly born; we offer you the way of truth.
In the beginning was the Great Spirit, the eternal one. But,
there was a second form, a desire for companionship. So, the
Great Spirit moved upon the face of the deep and created a
reflection of itself--the Word--the first manifestation. This
was the first creation. The Word was endowed with free will
and reason. It had purpose and was conscious of its oneness
with the creator."

Word, what is this Word? My consciousness shifted, an
uneasy balance of light and dark, sleep and non-sleep. The
use of symbols and myths intertwining. I began to dream,

20

thinking of the golden braids of a recent lover, then Sarah's
face, illuminated on the mountain. I drifted back to the
evening chill, shivered, and aroused to the guide's voice.

"The Word brought forth the inumerable souls which,
being created in the beginning by the reflection of the Great
Spirit, existed in perfect attunement. Possessing free will,
these souls created their own individuality. Every experience
became registered on the akashic records as well as upon the
soul as karma, but as each soul became fascinated with its
own creativity, selfishness came into being and from that the
destructive will and darkness--opposition to the goodness of
the Great Spirit, and there was an end to perfection. This
was the fall of emerging humanity."

Again a bathing light fell upon my body and I could sense
the filtered light of sunrise and the soft sweet smells of
morning.

"The Word, the first true being, saw what had happened
and was full of sorrow. Yet, a way was devised for these
separated souls to return to the truth.

"Within this world were created the Gods of daylight,
life, fertility, wisdom and good. Also, by reflection, were
created demons of darkness, death, barrenness and evil.

"The Great Spirit gave us the Gods symbolizing the
beneficial aspects of nature and the arts and intelligence
of humanity. These Gods were the first people, the first
of the perfect race. They were of only one sex. This event
occurred ten times ten times ten times ten thousand years
ago."

Mental calculations eased my shivering.

"When souls were created in the beginning, they were
neither male nor female but a unity. However, as the first
beings submerged themselves more and more into the material
world and its emphasis on the senses, humankind began losing
the powers of Gods."

Interesting . . . I began drifting again, absorbed in
my thoughts.

21

"Over all the earth at this time existed gigantic beasts,
kept in check by the mental control of humankind. There
also were animals which had been changed by genetic means into
the likeness of the people of the first world. These were
mental slaves."

A stirring, a primordial ancient stirring of rebellion,
against my own mental enslavement. Something subtle was
breaking loose in my thoughts.

"As humankind's control over these great beasts and
mental slaves disappeared, humankind attempted to destroy
the beasts. But, in doing so they unlocked the power of the
Earth Mother, which rose up and changed the structure of the
world. Mountains rose and fell. There were floods and great
destructions over all the earth plane, and this was the end
of the First World.

"In the beginning of the Second World, humankind
developed and became divided into male and female beings,
separated from unity but always with the desire to find unity
again. Humanity rose to great heights in the Second World,
but there were still greed and evil and a turning away from
the Great Spirit. The Word saw this and was saddened. Such
was the love of the Word for humankind, that it divided itself
even as humankind was divided, and of itself became one part
male and one part female, so that there was a duality. This
duality became the Lord and the Lady, the two in one, the
God/dess. But, humankind separated itself away from the Great
Spirit and the God/dess and perversion became rampant. There
were great disturbances within the Earth, as the mountains
wasted away. Many lands submerged and there was a great
burning time when even the water was aflame. The survivors
of these peoples migrated to other islands. This was the
end of the Second World."

Atlantis and Mu. I have not heard of Mu. There was a
sensation of the globe around us moving--huge shadows crawling
in toward a restless moonlight. A strangeness prevailing as

22

if I were being sucked backward, taken into darkness yet
without terror, nor in bonds.

"The deluge which submerged the lands in the Second World
was a time of great terror and destruction as whole oceans
left their boundaries to flow over the continents. The Earth
left its appointed path and took up a new station in the sky.
After the days of the second deluge, the Third World came into
being and this world was the greatest of all, for many true
people returned to worship the Great Spirit and the God/dess
of Nature, of wisdom and love. They captured the power of
the Sun in living stones and used it in the healing arts and
to power their world. They had great power of the mind and
could direct the forces of nature to do their bidding. They
built huge temples with the use of their minds and the odic
forces of the earth alone. But, again some of the humankind
turned to the material world to the exclusion of the spiritual
plane and humankind split into two factions; those who
believed in the Great Spirit and in the God/dess, the duality
of Nature, and those who followed selfishness whose powers
were those of death and destruction.

"Great battles insued and at the peak of their struggle,
the final destructions of the Third World took place. A
great wall of water came and submerged all the lands of the
two factions. This took place over twelve thousand years ago.
The result of this destruction was a great migration to other
lands. This was the end of the Third World."

Again, I shivered, then relaxed as a warmth spread back
over me.

"This is now the Fourth World. When the survivors of
the great deluge arrived in Wales, they merged with the inhabitants of the land. They brought with them the Secrets of Life
and Death and Rebirth, of the healing powers of the mind, and
of the powers of Mother Earth. These we will teach you."

My guide, Sarah, was with me on the weekends for almost
the entire eight months I was in Wales. Sometimes she could
stay longer, but very rarely. She taught me patiently,

23

openly, most of the knowledge which is passed from guide to
seeker, speaking as we walked along the meadow paths, but
the Elders taught all of us as a group.

The Elders were of varying ages, ranging from middle age
to well over eighty. They were both women and men, but their
complete lack of sexism made it easy to just call them "Elders."
When they were teaching they wore various colored robes
depending on their level of attainment. When they were working
it was difficult to tell them from anyone else in the community,
for when we were in the fields, we all wore common farm clothes.

At first it was forbidden to ask questions of the teachers.
"All will be explained at the proper time," was the standard
reply. This was of course very annoying to us, but it taught
us the valuable lesson of patience.

Sarah was speaking:

"William, you are one of the messengers of the Fifth
World, the world of completion. Your soul has entered back
into this world in order to teach those souls in need of
enlightenment. The message you will bring them is the
message of Love, Knowledge, and Power. Love for mankind,
Knowledge of Good, and Power over Life and Death.

"You will pass through many trials, you will overcome
many tribulations, and you will reach the state of enlightenment when you are needed. For the end of the Fourth World
is near. It will end in thirty-four more years. You must
be ready."

Sitting on the rocks in a stream, I looked at her as I
never had before, my eyes direct and understanding hers,
without the subtle shadowing looks as though always trying
to pick up loose threads or convey a sensuous whisper.

I had been chosen! I was going to do something important!

Little did I know at that time how much I was to learn
of "The Path."

24

CHAPTER TWO
The Symbolism of a Legend

25

CHAPTER TWO

THE LEGEND OF THE HIDDEN PEOPLE

"Men suppose, fancifully, that they know truth and divine perception. In fact they know nothing. . ." -Juzjani

Sarah was speaking seriously now--her tones harmonious, smooth. The legend she was telling was as ancient as the rocks in these northern Welsh hills.

"We have been hidden among Humanity from the beginning. We have been known by many names--Watchers, Fairy Folk, the Black Men, the Cunning Men--but all are names given by ourselves to hide the true message--that we are among Humanity for the benefit of mankind.

"At definite intervals there is a periodic destruction of this world. Our duty is to attempt to save what each cyclic culture creates and reveals of value in the physical and spiritual world. There is no way of controlling with certainty what is saved or how it is saved, but because at each period before each destruction, we have come forward to train the teachers, we have always succeeded in passing much knowledge through.

"Your duty as a teacher will be to learn all that is possible, to teach all that is possible, and to love all that is possible.

"When our people left Gwlad Yr Hav in the dying days of the old ones, our tribe of priests and priestesses, poets and teachers, traveled to all corners of the world. We took with us all our teachings in the form of the thirteen books of mystery and knowledge, it being our duty to preserve the knowledge of the ancients.

26

"We are of the Wicce people--we are of the Gnostics--
we are of the Hindus--we are of the Celts--we are of all
people. But, and yet, we are hidden within the race of man,
but not of the race of man. The world is the dwelling place
of man, but not the birthing place of man."

So many questions stirred within me. So why are you
hidden? What are you trying to do?

"We are hidden, my children, for our protection and for
the protection of our charges, humankind. We are forbidden
to teach directly, for as one of the masters said: 'Do not
cast what is valuable before those who can have no knowledge
of the value.' We carry the message of the secret of love,
knowledge and power.

"One day we will once again be called upon to teach.
When that time comes, secrecy shall be cast away. My children,
hold to your secrets within your heart and, no matter what
the provocation, use what you have knowledge of only for good
and not for evil. For the ones who seek us out would trap
you by your deeds, and would lie against you. Love all peoples,
teach your truths, and use your wisdom when the need arises.

"And that is the 'Legend of the Hidden Peoples,'" Sarah
was saying. "But it has a deeper meaning. It also is telling
you of the hidden teachings within all legends and myths."

"For example?" I said.

"Reincarnation is a good example. Within all major religions, even Christianity, is taught the doctrine of a
spiritual rebirth in a physical body after death. It is there
for all to see if they but have eyes to do so.

"William," she suddenly said, "tell me what you know
of reincarnation and karma."

I began, "At death, the soul passes to Gwlad Yr Hav, or
the Summerplace. This is a place of rest and adjustment, of
reunion with your loved ones." The recitation was almost
automatic.

"At this point, you meet with spirit guides and other
souls to choose your next incarnation. The life which is

The great hall

28

chosen is one which will teach you something necessary to your development." I paused for comment and when there was none, went on. "Gwlad Yr Hav, the Summerland, is the astral plane where the soul dwells between incarnations.

"Karma means 'action.' For every action there results an appropriate reaction, sooner or later. If this process is not worked out in one life, then it will be worked out in succeeding lives.

"Usually, there is no conscious memory of any previous life during the current one. The evolution of each soul continues by means of a series of human lives, until the physical plane is transcended."

"Right. You are doing very well," she said, smiling. This same doctrine was taught by our Celtic ancestors. As one of their doctrines, they believed that souls were not annihilated, but passed after death from one body to another, and they held that by this teaching men were encouraged to valour through disregarding the fear of death.

"The Greeks knew of it even before the time of Rome. The doctrine of Pythagoras prevailed among them, according to which the souls of men were immortal and, after a fixed term, recommenced to live, taking upon themselves a new body."

"What other 'hidden teachings' are known?"

She smiled at me, seeing I suppose, a new curiosity emerge from the harder core of skepticism.

"Another good example would be the knowledge of the seven planes of existence in the universe. These have been passed down as the seven days of the week, the seven heavens, and as many other symbols. In reality, they are seven distinct planes or dimensions of existence which have their own atoms and molecules, but each plane is vibrating at a different cosmic rate. Therefore, they can coexist in the same 'space.' These are the physical plane, the etheric plane, the astral plane, the mental plane, the spiritual plane, the duality plane, and the celestial plane. When your body dies or stops functioning, your soul, with your personality,

emerges and immediately sets out for the etheric plane.
Unfortunately, sometimes, if the soul is not properly enlightened, it will wish to stay in the physical or earth
plane until convinced otherwise. We are taught that death
is a very pleasant experience. For the majority, the soul
transcends this physical plane, where it rests."

"What is the etheric plane?"

"The etheric plane contains a matrix pattern of all life
on the physical plane. This matrix pattern is the vital body
and duplicates your body exactly in every way. This pattern
is what determines your physical makeup. It is also perceived
as the 'aura.'

"The astral plane, as you have learned, is that place that
the ancients called Gwlad Yr Hav--the Summerland. It is also
called 'heaven' by some, and 'hell' by others."

"What do you mean by this?" I asked curiously.

"The astral plane has various levels. The upper levels
are inhabited by those souls who are following the true pathway to enlightenment. It is beautiful beyond belief and is
a proper resting place between incarnations. But, the lower
levels are for those base souls who not only make their own
hell on earth, but carry it with them. It is a vile place,
full of fear and depravity."

"How does a soul arrive at a particular level?" I asked.

"Karma," she replied, "as you know, is a law which
states that for every action there will be an appropriate reaction, and as I stated before, this reaction may come in this
life or the next, but it will come. These actions and reactions, or deeds, become a part of the akashic record which is
located on the etheric plane.

"The akashic record is a pattern and records all events.
But, since it is not governed by time, both past and future
events may be found there."

"You mean that if I could somehow contact it, I could
know the future?"

"Or the past," she said. "In fact, that is what precognition and clairvoyance are, an extrasensory awareness of the akashic records."

"What about telepathy?" I asked.

"Telepathy is different," she replied. "It is tuning into the mental field of another person."

"How about the rest of the planes?"

"Well, the mental plane, which is above the astral, is where the masters live."

"Who are they?" I asked.

"They are those souls who have reached enlightenment of the highest order and are waiting for the rest of humanity to catch up. We are taught that their mental power is such that they could vaporize the entire earth with their collective will. But, of course, they have risen above such things. They are more interested in helping humanity improve itself. These masters from time to time contact selected individuals in their attempt to help direct humanity to the right pathway."

"Are these the same masters that are mentioned in various religions such as Buddah and Jesus?"

"No! Definitely not," she answered. "Those entities were reincarnated for the specific purpose of providing a host for one of the entities on the spiritual plane, who from time to time come to this plane to give humankind the message of peace and love. Jesus was such a one who provided the host for Melchezidek, the Lord of Light, also known by the Christians as Christ.

"These entities come to this plane to give us a sign and communicate directly. They are perfected beings, who although inhabiting physical bodies, are spiritual in nature. They teach us by example and reveal the mystery of love.

"Melchezidek is the Ruler of the sixth plane."

"But what about the Lady? It seems as though most of the deities and masters that I have ever read about have been male. Where does the female come in?"

31

"William, the universe runs in cycles and there is an attempt by karmic law to balance everything out. Of course, absolute balance is never reached, but there is a seeking for this balance by every atom of every plane in every universe. It's the same with civilizations and societies. We have been living at the end of a patriarchal cycle of this world. The new cycle is beginning. It will at first be somewhat balanced, for the first thousand years, according to our teachings, but it will gradually change to a complete matriarchy and women will rule society. But, more of this later."

"What do you mean later?" I said with indignation. "Here you are making an important statement on the future of the human race and you stop in the middle!"

"Later, William," she said patiently. "First things first. You asked a question and haven't heard the answer yet.

"The fifth or spiritual plane is that which contains the deities known by some as angels and others by archetypal symbols of creation. These beings created the various planets in their solar system and each planet has an angelic host and planetary guardian. For instance, the planet, Earth, has a guardian known as Earth Mother by some and Jehovah by others.

"Above the spiritual plane is the plane of duality. This is the abode of those entities known as the Lord and Lady; the God and Goddess; the male and female aspects of the Great Spirit. These are the forces who we worship, and by worshipping, give them power. Remember William that all power rises on the planes, ultimately going to the Great Spirit who resides on the celestial plane.

"Of the upper three planes, we know very little, only what the adepts and masters tell us. But, we can experience the lower four, and we do this by meditating and learning concentration. For our task is to learn all there is to know about the four lowest planes through trial and error and seeking enlightenment. The ultimate goal, of course, is being one with the Great Spirit."

32

"And, what about sex?"

"What do you mean, William?"

"I mean, what are the precepts on sexual conduct among the beautiful family?"

"William, sex as a personal experience, cannot be regulated by law or rules, but it is a sacred part of our religious life. Therefore, we can teach the correct use of it in that context. The only law which is unchangeable is: "If it harms no one, do what you will." But 'harm' must be used in the broad sense of mental harm, spiritual harm, or physical harm. In other words, think before you act. We are not trying to take away your spontaneity of expression, but when you accepted our religion as your own, you also accepted certain basic concepts of reincarnation, karma, and the male and female duality of the Great Spirit.

"Sex is part of that duality. Therefore, if you use sex for pleasure at the expense of someone else's feelings, you are accepting the karmic consequences. As long as two people accept the sexual act as a joyous, wonderful experience, free from guilt, their act hurts no one. They are free to do as they wish. But once guilt enters their minds, there could be injury. It is recommended that two people not become sexually involved without exploring the possibility of harm and guilt.

"William, sex is a natural part of our lives and should be accepted as such. Unfortunately, most people in our society are raised with the idea that sex is dirty--that sex is evil, and that one must refrain from all pleasure of the body in order to become enlightened.

"That concept is wrong. Sex is beautiful and a wonderful expression of our love and friendship for our fellow brothers and sisters."

She looked wryly at me. Don't worry, Rhuddlwm, if you intentionally harm anyone by the use of sex, although karmic law will see that you feel the reaction to that hurt, you will also be severely censored by your Elders!"

"Sarah, I have noticed that there seems to be more female than male Guides in the village. Does this mean there are more females than males in our clan?"

"William, if you saw three red fishing boats than one blue boat out on the bay, would you then think by observation that three out of four of all fishing boats were red?"

"No."

"You have answered your own question."

"Well, why, then are there more females than males?"

"Because throughout Nature there is a seeking of balance. Women have been enslaved, maligned, raped and otherwise degraded throughout the last two thousand years. In effect, the pendulum has swung to the right, the masculine side, and the world has been in a patriarchial cycle.

"During this, the Aquarian Age, the pendulum will begin its swing to the left, the feminine side, and the world will begin a matriarchal cycle."

I thought for several minutes. "But, if females have been downtrodden during a patriarchal age, does that mean that males will experience the same fate in a matriarchal culture?"

"Maybe."

"But is that just?" I asked.

"No, not any more than what man has done to woman in the past ages. But that is a matter of karma, for always remember that for every action there will be a reaction. Man as an entity must pay the karmic debt he owes women."

"Will it ever stop?" I asked sadly.

"Only when humankind stands back, objectively looks at the pendulum as it swings and decides that enough is enough.

"There are more female guides, William, because you as a male have had it drummed into your head from childhood that men are stronger than women, that men are smarter than women, that men are in all ways superior to women. If this condition was allowed to continue, you would not be able to teach the way of truth."

34

"But I think I'm a fair person, Elder. I know that women are my equal," I said with concern.

"Yes, William, I believe that you think so. But this is only true on a conscious level. Unconsciously you still evidence male superiority characteristics which are unacceptable."

"How?" I asked with exasperation.

"You are patronizing in your manner. You still try to play the same old games of warrior male conquering the defenseless female. William, you must be able to relate to your fellow seekers as absolute equals no matter what their sex. You must not allow so called male pride to get in the way of asking a female for help if you need it. In your romantic life, when a woman says no, that is what she means. You must respect that decision on her part. For you, a seeker of Y Tylwyth Teg, you must never again play games with people's minds. They will attempt to play games with you, but you must not give in to that temptation. Females have been taught that they are fair game and you, the hunter, are attempting to capture them physically, and mentally. This is animal instinct which humankind uses in the game of civilization.

"That is why there are more female guides. That is why, wherever you turn, there is a female within sight, one who is superior to you in knowledge and in training. We are attempting to balance your mind in its thinking, to deprogram you and to re-link you with Mother Earth and your sisters.

"Remember, William, we are here to preserve the knowlege for humanity after the next devastation. The knowledge of male and female equality and balance must be preserved if we are to establish the new order of truth."

The wind which had started picking up along the darkened ridges, pushed down through the gulleys and the few trees silvered their leaves with twisting, snapping shapes against the moving dark wedges of clouds.

35

"The universal wisdom of the philosophy taught by Y Tylwyth Teg has long attracted the more advanced souls of the world to its pathway. Y Tylwyth Teg has gathered seekers from the ranks of all religions of the world, as well as from among scientists, artists, free thinkers, housewives, truck drivers, and laborers from all strata of society. Seekers with the virtues of goodwill, honesty, and humility have always been sought out as candidates for the 'ordeal.' Each seeker was contacted by Y Tylwyth Teg when the philosophy provided by our culture failed to give the seeker what was needed. The seeker hungered for the deeper answers which heretofore had been lacking. But, the seeker must also have advanced enough to discard dogma and be capable of embracing truth; not ordinary truth but that truth which can survive every test.

"Because of the rigorous screening process, it is no wonder that no seeker has yet violated the rigid code of group secrecy which must be honored. To all outward appearances, each seeker continues to live a normal life, keeping former friends and associates, but it becomes obvious to friends and relatives after a few years that something astounding is occurring. This individual has acquired personal serenity, courage, strength of character, and self control, and has become an outstanding and successful member of society. That person will have become an oracle of wisdom and an island of peace in this vast ocean of struggling humanity.

"The seeker's success in acquiring spiritual peace and happiness reflects the careful selection of Y Tylwyth Teg in choosing candidates for 'the ordeal.' For over one thousand years, Y Tylwyth Teg has very carefully and quietly built up a select membership. The activities of these seekers are now for the first time being made public. It is extremely important because of the geological as well as sociological condition of the earth.

"The earth will soon undergo a cataclysmic change in its physical makeup. Continents will become flooded and new land will appear out of the sea. The oldest religion will become the new religion. The cycle is beginning anew.

"In order to raise yourself from the physical to the astral dimension, you must give up traditional concepts of evil. You must expand your sense of love, of health, and of understanding. You must also learn to contact those parts of your being that are male and those parts that are female, for both exist regardless of the sex of your body.

"The primary aim of all those who follow our pathway is enlightenment. And, what is enlightenment? It is the realization of your oneness with the Great Spirit, but it does not come as a gift of knowledge. It comes, rather, as a mystical experience.

"The true evidence of God/dess is unknown. We see the Lord and the Lady as a symbol of our visualization of the God/dess, as a symbol of the evolution of the soul. For, humankind is eternally attempting to return to the creator and in the process of this journey one is reincarnated to learn and experience certain lessons, these lessons being important to the soul's progression.

"To Y Tylwyth Teg, everything is a matrix of balancing opposites—the equilibriating process. This is energy. This is life.

"In your daily life, at any given moment, you have a multitude of choices of action, some trivial and some of extreme importance. You may laugh or not, go swimming or read, talk, walk, or sit, harm someone or turn the other cheek. In your choice you fix reality by making that choice a physical action instead of a possibility. We, of the Hidden People, are here to help you determine your choice."

CHAPTER 3
"SARAH"

CHAPTER THREE

WHY?

"Assuredly there is a price to knowledge. It is to
be given only to those who can keep it and not use
it. . ." -Ikrima

We gathered around as the Bard began to speak. "We are
not here in order to gratify your desire for truth. We are
here to show you a pathway which will lead you to that which
you are seeking."
"Why?" one of the newest ones asked.
"Why, what?" smiled the Bard as she turned to the seeker,
understanding that initial frustration of each new class of
seekers.
"Why can't you gratify our desire for truth?" stammered
the new seeker.
"Innocent one, listen to the story of Why!" She spoke
with sparkling eyes:

*   *   *   *

One night while sitting on the moon, I leaned over grasping the west pointing horn of it, and looked down. Against
the other horn a Shining One reclined motionless and looked
across at me.
Below me, the hills and valleys were thick with Cymmry,
and the moon swung low that I might see them. 'Who are they?'
I asked the Shining One, for I was unafraid.
'They are the sons and daughters of the Infinite One,'
answered the Shining One.
I looked again and saw that they beat and trampled one
another and sometimes they didn't seem to know when one of

their fellow creatures whom they pushed from their path
fell under their feet. But, sometimes, they did look and
kicked him brutally.

I looked up at the Shining One. 'Are they all the
sons and daughters of the Infinite One?'

And the Shining One answered, 'All.'

I leaned over again and it grew clear to me as I watched
them that each one was frantically seeking something, and that
it was because they sought what they sought with such single-
ness of purpose that they were so inhuman to all who hindered
them. 'What do they seek?' I asked the Shining One.

'Happiness.'

'Are they all seeking happiness?'

'All.'

'Have any of them found it?'

'None of those have found it.'

'Do they ever think that they have found it?'

'Sometimes they think they have found it.'

My eyes filled with tears, for at this moment I caught
a glimpse of a woman with a babe at her breast, and I saw
the babe torn from her arms and the woman was cast into a
deep pit by a man whose eyes were fixed on a shining yellow
lump that he believed to be, or possibly to contain, I know
not which, happiness.

And I turned to the Shining One. My eyes were blinded.
'Will they ever find it?'

And he said, 'They will find it.'

'All of them?'

'All of them.'

'Those who are trampled?'

'Those who are trampled.'

'And those who trample?'

'And those who trample.'

I looked again for a long time at what they were doing
on the hills and in the valleys and again my eyes were

blinded with tears. And I sobbed out to the Shining One,
'Is it the Gods' will, or the work of a devil that humankind
seeks happiness?'

'It is the Gods' will.'

'But, it looks so like the work of a devil.'

The Shining One smiled inscrutably. 'It does look like
the work of a devil, doesn't it?'

When I had looked a while longer, I cried out protesting,
'Why have they been put down there to seek happiness and to
cause each other such immeasurable misery?'

Again the Shining One smiled inscrutably. 'They are
learning.'

'What are they learning?'

'They are learning life, and they are learning love.'

I said nothing. One man in the herd below held me
breathless. Fascinated, I watched as bound, struggling bodies
of living men were laid before him, that he might tread upon
them and never touch foot to earth. Proudly he strode over
them, but suddenly a whirlwind seized him, tore his purple
robe from him, and set him down, naked among strangers.
They fell on him and maltreated him sorely. I clapped my
hands. 'Good! Good! I cried excitedly. 'He got what he
deserved.'

Then I looked up suddenly and saw again the inscrutable
smile of the Shining One who spoke quietly. 'They all get
what they deserve.'

'And no worse?' I asked incredulously.

'No worse.'

'And no better?'

'How can there be any better? They each deserve whatever shall teach them the true way to happiness.'

I was silenced. And still the people went on seeking
and trampling each other in their eagerness to find, and I
perceived what I had not fully grasped before. That the
wind, seemingly without design, caught them up from time to

time and set them down elsewhere to continue the search.
And, I said to the Shining One, 'Does the whirlwind always
set them down again on these hills and in these valleys?'

And the Shining One said, 'Not always on these hills and
in these valleys.'

'Where, then?'

'Look above you.'

And I looked up. Above me stretched the Milky Way and
gleaming stars. And I breathed, 'Oh,' and fell silent,
awed by what was given me to comprehend. Below me, they
still trampled each other. And I asked the Shining One,
'But, no matter where the whirlwind sets them down, they go on
seeking happiness?'

'They go seeking happiness.'

'And the whirlwind makes no mistakes?'

'The whirlwind makes no mistakes.'

'It puts them down sooner or later where they will get
what they deserve?'

'This is so.'

Then the load crushing my heart lightened, and I found
I could look at the brutal cruelties that went on below me
with pity for the cruel, and the longer I looked, the stronger
the compassion grew. And I said to the Shining One, 'They
act like men goaded.'

'They are goaded.'

'Who goads them?'

'The name of the goad is desire.'

Then, when I had looked a while longer, I cried out
passionately, 'Desire is an evil thing.'

But the face of the Shining One grew stern and his voice
rang out, dismaying me. 'Desire is not an evil thing!'

I trembled and thought, withdrawing myself into the innermost chamber of my heart till at last I said, 'It is desire
that nerves men to learn the lessons the Gods have set?'

'This is so.'

'The lessons of life and love?'

'The lessons of life and love.'

Then I could no longer see that they were cruel.
I could only see that they were learning. I watched them
with deep love and compassion as one by one, the whirlwind
carried them out of sight.

*   *   *   *   *

As the Bard ended her story, we sat silently, each
lost in thought. After a while, a sandy haired guy with a
handwoven sweater spoke out.

"What you are saying then is that we should just allow
the uncertainties of life to take us where it will and not do
anything about it."

"Not quite," the Bard laughed rather cryptically, making
us all ill at ease.

Cowed, the new seeker cringed and tried to hide behind
the others.

"Innocent one," said the Bard. "Have your experiences
here meant so little to you? William, you try to pull a
needle through the weave of the story."

"Oh no," I groaned inwardly. I felt she was testing
me. I was still trying to work with memory and logic,
trying to grasp details in a sensible way. "I'm not sure
where to begin. There is just so much sybmolism," I stammered.

"Symbolism, huh?" the Bard snorted.

"The whirlwind does symbolize the uncertainties of life,"
I began a little stronger.

"Yes-s-s," she said thoughtfully. "But is that the real
essence of the story? Isn't there more to it?"

"Yes," I said. "To me, this story communicates the
unknowable aspects of the Great Spirit and the God and Goddess.
It shows that no matter what our action, we will receive our
just reward."

"Do you think the story proves the concept of reincarnation?" said the Bard, her eyes twinkling.

"No," I said confidently. "The story doesn't prove anything any more than the Christian Bible proves that the world was created in seven days. But, it does give a seeker food for thought which will help that seeker in the search for truth."

The Bard looked at the lanky kid who had spoken first with a kindly expression. "If you remember anything, remember to look deeper into those things that may seem simple at first."

The young novice nooded, still fumbling a bit with confusion.

The Bard turned to me. "And, William, don't become so caught up in symbolism that you forget to feel and experience with your heart as well as with your head. The symbolism will eventually be understood."

She addressed all of us. "The meaning of the story is not simple. You must look at all actions and all incidents of life as a communication from the God and Goddess. When you have learned to understand those messages, you will have succeeded in raising your consciousness just that much higher, and your soul will experience those things which are needed for progression. Therefore, if it seems that you are getting more than your share of misfortune, don't despair, for the lessons are more important than the incidents. Try to do only good works and you will help to balance out the karmic debts of past lives. And ever remember the law of the threefold return--'Whatever is done, returns to the doer threefold.'"

That night, exhausted from the day's work, I lay on my pallet and thought of the story. And as our guide's words came back to me, I began to see that although the story was only a story, the ideas that it generated were endless: Man's inhumanity to man; the uncertainties of life; reincarnation; the concept of the Godhead; the Divine Plan. They were all represented in the story, and I began to see that our guide was correct as usual. "Feel the experience first and don't get so caught up in the symbolism. The symbolism will come later."

It's been over eleven years now since I first heard that story. I have yet to completely investigate all of its many concepts.

CHAPTER 4
The Pathway of Enlightenment

CHAPTER FOUR

THE MABINOGION

"The narratives of the doctrine are its cloak. The
simple look only on the garment. . . more they know
not. The instructured, however, see not merely the
cloak, but what the cloak covers." -Franck

Our bardic teacher was speaking of olden times:
"We of the tribe of Dynwyn Myn have the keys to these
mystic tales which you will eventually learn and then
memorize.

"Long ago, when our bardic ancestors underwent strict
poetic training in order to master the traditional lore of
the ancients, these novice seekers were called the 'Mabinog.'
These tales are representative of the many mystical and
sacred tales of the Cymmry.

"By means of a mnemonic system, thousands of lines of
poetry were memorized word for word by ancient seekers of
truth. It was a requirement that over one hundred and forty-
seven poems be memorized word perfect.

"In those days it was considered a sacriledge to put
words into letters or signs, so all poems and prose writings
were orally transmitted from guide to seeker. This 'Literature' contained all the archetypal knowledge which aided the
seeker in reaching the goal of 'Enlightenment.'

"Today we still teach the mnemonic technique of memory
training, but, sadly, only as an aid--our poems and lore are
widely printed and profaned in books in many languages not
of the purest translation.

"The first of the three tales you will study is that of
Math vab Mathonwy. This is the story of 'the dying God' who

47

dies in the winter month with his place taken by a rival, and then is reborn a year later. This legend teaches of the mysteries of the life giving Sun, reincarnation, and contains knowledge of initiation."

She paused for a moment, and her eyes got a far away look within them.

"Here then is the tale of Math vab Mathonwy:

* * * * *

"Arianrhod, the daughter of the Goddess Don and the niece of Math, had a son by her brother Gwydion. Being of a cold nature, Arianrhod would not care for her offspring, so Gwydion, the lad's father, brought him up.

"One day he and Gwydion met his mother, Arianrhod, while walking in the forest. She prophesied and declared that her son should be nameless until she herself gave him a name, which she refused to do. But, using trickery, Gwydion obtained from Arianrhod the name of Llew Lawgyfies for his son (Lion of the Cunning Hand). Later she declared that he should never receive armor unless she herself gave it to him. But, again, Gwydion accomplished the impossible and obtained arms for Llew at the hands of Arianrhod. The third time, Arianrhod declared that her son would never obtain a wife 'of the race that now inhabits the Earth' and once again Gwydion thwarted her desires with the help of Math, who was a great magician. Gwydion created a wife of the blossoms of the oak, the broom, and the meadowsweet. Her name was Blodeuwedd, or 'Flowerface.'

"One day while Llew was away from the palace, Mur Y Castell, which was on the confines of Ardudwy, Goronwy Pevr, the Lord of Penllyn, who had been a-hunting stag until late in the day, sought shelter for the night at Mur Y Castell. He remained three days and feel in love with Blodeuwedd.

"So great was this love that they felt for one another that they plotted to kill Llew. By questioning Llew at the direction of Goronwy, Blodeuwedd learned that he could only be killed by making a bath for him by the side of the river and by putting a roof over the vat, thatching it well and

tightly, and bringing a goat and putting it beside the vat.
Then, if he placed one foot on the goat's back and the other
on the edge of the vat, whosoever struck him would cause his
death. The spear by which he was to be struck would require
a year to be made.

"Blodeuwedd revealed this to Goronwy who set to work
making the spear. When it was ready, Blodeuwedd prevailed
upon Llew to show her the exact position in which he could be
slain. He did so, and Goronwy who was hiding on a hill,
flung the poisoned spear and pierced him in the side. Llew
gave a fearful scream and taking the form of an eagle, flew
upward, thenceforth no more to be seen. Goronwy and Blodeuwedd
took possession of the lands.

"The story continues and tells us that Math and Gwydion
grieved. Gwydion declared that he would not rest until he
knew the fate of Llew. One day Gwydion discovered an eagle
at the top of an oak tree near a brook now called the 'Lion's
Brook,' and after three attempts persuaded it, a mass of ver-
min and putrid flesh, to come down until it settled on
Gwydion's knee. With a touch of his magic wand, Gwydion re-
stored Llew to his own form, but he was nothing but skin and
bone. By the end of the year, Llew had recovered and planned
his revenge for what he had suffered.

"Gwydion then went to Mur Y Castell to confront
Blodeuwedd. When she heard he was coming, she took her
maidens and fled. They passed through the river Cynvad and
went towards a court that was upon the mountain. Through fear,
they could not proceed except with their faces looking back-
wards, so, unaware, they fell into the lake. They were all
drowned except Blodeuwedd, who was changed by Gwydion into
an owl for her sins--the owl 'which dares not show its face
in the light of day, and is always hateful to all birds.'

"Meanwhile, Goronwy withdrew to Penllyn whre he suffered
death in exactly the same way and in the same spot as Llew.
He asked to place a stone between himself and the blow, but

the spear pierced both the slab and Goronwy and so he
died."

*   *   *   *   *

A beautiful tale, I mused. I could imagine the story
being told in these upland plateaus for centuries, the words
echoing in the hills and running with the clear streams near
the villages.   But I still was trying to get at the larger
significance--the relationship to the whole experience of
life and death.

"Elder, how does this story relate to the Sun, and the
Earth, and Life?" I asked.

"William, the Earth is the Mother and during ancient
times, the dying plant was thought of as her consort who
yearly had to perish in order that he might give life to
his son. But, the Earth appeared to grow old as Autumn passed,
giving place to Winter and the thought that she might die and
cease to be able to provide food caused the ancients to try
to help her through this dangerous time and to recover her
youth once more.

"The consort perished after passing on to his son the
divine soul, just as the seed pod must die before it can bring
forth more corn. We can compare this with the practice of the
Priests of Nemi, the kings of the wood. This grove, a
sanctuary, was sacred to Diana and there grew a certain tree
round which at any time of the day, and probably into the
night, a grim figure might be seen to prowl. In his hand he
carried a drawn sword, and he kept peering eerily about him
as if at any moment he expected to be set upon by an enemy.
He was a priest and a murderer, and the man for whom he looked
was sooner or later to murder him and hold the priesthood in
his stead. Such was the rule of the sanctuary. A candidate
for the priesthood could only succeed by slaying the priest,
and this he could not do until he had plucked the bough of a
certain tree in the grove. Having slain him, the murderer
retained office until he himself was slain by a stronger and
more cunning candidate.

50

"Llew is the Celtic representative of the God who annually died that the earth might bring forth her fruit and cause the flocks to increase. He is the same as the ancient god, Tammuz, Adonis, Horus, and Osiris."

"Oh, I see!" I exclaimed. "The same god in different aspects represents the Sun, the Moon, or the Spirit of Vegetation."

"Yes," she replied. "For instance, in many legends, Tammuz tends to become closely identified with the Moon and Astarte with Venus, while the Sun is hostile to his lover.

"Llew in these legends can represent both Corn God and Sun God. His name itself reveals the symbol of light--Llew meaning 'Light.' He is also the symbol of the winter solstice as he is found standing with one foot on the vat (Aquarius) and the other on the back of a goat (Capricorn). Between the two the winter solstice, or the month between December twenty-first and January twenty-first, is the birth of the Sun."

My brain began spinning at these new concepts.

"The rest of the legend involving the marriage of sister and brother, Gwydion and Arianrhod, children of the Goddess Don, contains the symbolism of initiation. The God had no proper name and seekers can identify with him as newly born without proper names. This is the 'naming.'

"Iron tools may not be brought into the presence of the human representative of the vegetation god, because to display the cause of the future death of vegetation before its incarnate god would obviously be an insult. The 'quest' is the search for arms and the power over life.

"Arianrhod as the Great Mother was also mother and consort of the God and could tolerate no rival. Therefore, she declared that Llew should have no wife from among the race then living, meaning of course, never. Blodeuwedd is only Arianrhod in another respect--as Goddess of vegetation. The marriage with Blodeuwedd represents the 'adoption' or sacred marriage between the seeker and the family or clan."

51

Several nights later, Sarah and I were walking along the stream and she asked me to sit down and watch the moon. We didn't talk but just sat there for a long time. My mind drifted back to the lessons of the past few days--thoughts of the Cycle of Life, nature, reincarnation, and magick. I recalled the tale told the night before: Pwyll, Prince of Dyved--another tale of the Mabinogion and another type of seasonal folktale.

* * * * *

"Pwyll was lord of the seven cantrevs of Dyved. Once while out hunting the stag in the wood near Glyn Cuch, he encountered another hunter whose dogs had pulled down the same stag he was hunting.

"He drove the strange dogs away and set his own dogs upon the stag.

"A horseman clad in grey rode up and accused Pwyll of gross discourtesy for robbing him of the kill, whereupon Pwyll asked him his name and what he could do to repair the damage done to the stranger's honor.

"He replied that his name was Arawn, a king of Annwyn, and that if Pwyll wished to gain his friendship, he should rid Arawn of a rival king, Havgan, who had been warring against him. 'Gladly will I do this," replied Pwyll. Arawn then changed his form into that of Pwyll and Pwyll into the form of Arawn and sent the transformed Pwyll in his place back to the kingdom of Annwyn.

"There, in the palace of Arawn, Pwyll subdued Havgan, the rival king, in a magical battle at the end of a year, and also conquered the rest of Annwyn. He then returned to Glyn Cuch and Arawn gave Pwyll, Prince of Dyved, his proper form and took himself his own. And so well had each ruled in the others stead that they became friends and gave gifts to one another."

I interrupted cautiously. "Is this a transformation myth?"

"No," she answered. "The main symbolism in this part of the Mabinogion is the two Gods exchanging places each year.

52

The battle with Havgan represents the death of the Sun during the winter and its renewal at the end of the season."

The words of our teacher seemed to float back and blend with the soft evening sounds of the breeze brushing against the mossy boulders.

"Pwyll was at Narberth, his chief palace, and while on the top of Gorsedd Arbeth, a mound near the palace, he observed a beautiful lady on a pure white horse. She seemed to be traveling at a slow pace, but when he sent runners to bring her to him, she always seemed to be further ahead. The same thing happened when he sent horsemen, and the fastest horses could not catch her even though she went at a slow pace.

"Finally, he himself went after her on the fastest horse in his possession, but fared no different than the rest. So he called after her and asked her to stop, whereupon she did, and told him her name and her errand. Her name was Rhiannon and she was seeking him because her father sought to give her to a husband against her will, and would he help her.

"Since she was very beautiful, he immediately fell in love with her, whereupon he told her that 'If I might choose among all the ladies and damsels in the world, tis thee I would choose' and he agreed to help her. They decided to meet at her father's castle a year hence, at which time he would ask for her hand and attend the wedding feast.

"At the end of the year he arrived at her father's castle so as to partake of the wedding feast. But a strange youth approached him and asked a boon of him, and because he was feeling so good he replied, 'What boon soever thou mayst ask of me, so far as I am able, thou shalt have.' The stranger was, of course, the rejected suitor her father was going to marry her to.

"He was forced by honor to bestow Rhiannon on the young suitor, whose name was Gwawl Ap Cluch, but Rhiannon told Pwyll that she would never be Gwawl's, and that at the end of the twelve month engagement period, Pwyll was to return and bring a bag with him. The bag was of such a nature that it could not be filled unless a man of noble birth pressed the food in the bag with both his feet.

"At the end of twelve months, Pwyll presented himself at the feast dressed in rags and asked for food to be placed in his bag. But the bag could not be filled. Gwawl then stepped into the bag to press it down, whereupon Pwyll pulled the bag up over Gwawl, tied it, and cast him into prison.

"Gwawl was released after a time, but only after he had returned Rhiannon to Pwyll."

I smiled as I thought of this part of the story--of Rhiannon as the Moon, on the pure white horse, unable to be caught however fast she was chased.

"Sarah," I said.

She turned to look toward me, the trees sketching shadows on her moonlit face.

"I think the moon is closer tonight. It might even drop in the stream like a lucky coin."

We laughed. Then she looked back up to the hills and her face was once more shadowed. I began to retrace symbolism again.

"In this portion of the Mabinogion, Rhiannon represents the Moon, 'who could not be caught no matter how fast she was chased.' Again we have seasonal symbolism of the Sun, Pwyll, fighting over the Moon, Rhiannon, with the year as the symbol of the complete cycle of nature.

"The remainder of the story tells of the birth of Pryderi, son of Rhiannon, his disappearance, and recovery at the end of four years. This is symbolic of the disappearance and return of the Moon at the end of four quarters.

"Reincarnation, balance, the cycle of nature, and the use of magick, as demonstrated by these tales, have been passed down from guide to seeker for thousands of years. In this way, we have hidden the sacred knowledge in fables and folk tales and have never lost it."

54

By this time our studies had taken us to some of the most remarkable legends in the life of mankind, and a sense of the universality of the tales had developed. Where and how these stories originated intrigued us all. The intricacy and complexity of them was part of the mystery. One other tale unfolded as part of the fabulous Mabinogion group. The "Mystical Cauldron of Cerridwen" also tells of initiation in its hidden passages rich with symbolism.

* * * * *

"In former times, there was a man of noble descent in Penllyn, the end of the lake. His name was Tegid Voel, and his paternal estate, Pemble Meer, was in the middle of the Lake of Tegid.

"His espoused wife was named Cerridwen. By this wife he had a son, named Morvrap Ap Tegid, 'Raven of the Sea,' the Son of Serenity, and a daughter called Criervyw, the 'Sacred Token of Life.' She was the most beautiful damsel in the world. But these children had a brother named Avagddu, 'Utter Darkness,' or black accumulation, the most hideous of beings.

"Cerridwen, the mother of this deformed son, concluded in her mind that he would have but little chance of being admitted into respectable company unless he were endowed with some honorable accomplishments or abilities. She determined, by consulting the mystery books of Pheryllt, to prepare for her son a Cauldron of Awen a Gwyboden, 'Water of Inspiration and Science,' that he might be more readily admitted into honorable society, upon account of his knowledge and his skill at prophecy.

"The Cauldron began to boil and it was required that the boiling should be continued without interruption for the period of a year and a day till three drops of the blessed endowment of the Spirit could be obtained.

"In Cair Einiawn, 'the City of the Just,' located in Powys, 'the Land of Rest,' she had stationed Gwion the Little,

55

the son of Gwreang the Herald, of Llanvair to superintend
the preparation of the Cauldron, and she had appointed a
blind man named Morde, Ruler of the Sea, to kindle the fire
under the Cauldron, with strict injunction that he should not
suffer the boiling to be interrupted before the completion
of the year and a day.

"Meanwhile, Cerridwen, with due attention to the books
of Astrology, and to the Hours of the Planets, employed herself daily in collecting plants of every species which pos-
sessed rare virtues.

"On a certain day, about the completion of a year, whilst
she was botanizing and muttering to herself, three drops of
the efficacious liquid happened to fly out of the Cauldron
and light upon the finger of Gwion the Little who was
watching the Cauldron. The heat of the water occasioned
him putting his finger in his mouth.

"As soon as these precious drops had touched his lips,
every event of the future was opened to his view. And, he
instantly perceived that his greatest concern was to beware
of the vengeance of Cerridwen, whose knowledge was very great.
With extreme terror, he fled toward his native country.

"As for the Cauldron, it divided itself in half, for
the whole of the water which it contained, except for those
three efficacious drops was poisonous. Emptying into a
channel, the Cauldron waters poisoned the horses of Gwyddns
Garanhir which had come to drink there. Hence, the channel
was afterwards called 'the Poison of Gwyddns Horses.'

"Cerridwen, entering just at this moment and perceiving
that her whole year's labour was entirely lost, seized an
oar and struck the blind Morde upon his head so that one of
his eyes dropped upon his cheek.

"'Thou has disfigured me wrongfully!' exclaimed Morde.
'Thy loss has not been occasioned by any fault of mine.'

"'True,' replied Cerridwen, 'it was Gwion the Little who
robbed me.' Having pronounced these words, she began to run
in pursuit of him.

"Gwion, perceiving her at a distance, transformed himself into a hare and doubled his speed, but Cerridwen instantly becoming a greyhound bitch, turned him, and chased him toward a river.

"Leaping into the stream, he assumed the form of a fish, but Cerridwen became an otter bitch and teased him through the stream so that he was obliged to take the form of a bird and mount into the air.

"That element afforded him no refuge, for the Lady, in the form of a sparrow hawk, was gaining upon him. She was just about to pounce on him when, shuddering with the dread of death, he perceived a heap of clean wheat upon the floor, dropped into the midst of it, and assumed the shape of a single grain.

"Cerridwen, taking the form of a black crested hen, descended into the wheat, scratched him out, distinguished him, and swallowed him. And, as the history relates, she was pregnant with him nine months and when she gave birth found him so lovely a babe that she had not the resolution to put him to death.

"She placed him, however, in a coracle, a small hooped boat covered with a skin, and by the instigation of her husband, cast him into the sea on the twenty-ninth of April.

"In those days, Gwyddono's weir stood out in the beach between Dyvic and Abergstwyth near his own castle. And in that age it was usual to take fish, to the value of a hundred pounds, every year upon the first of May.

"Gwyddno had only one son named Elphin, a most unfortunate young man. This was a great affliction to his father, who began to think that his son had been born in an evil hour.

"His counselors, however, persuaded the father to let this son have the result from the drawing of the weir (net) on this year by way of an experiment in order to prove whether any good fortune would ever attend him, and that he might have something with which to enter the world.

"The next day being May Eve, Elphin examined the weir and found nothing, but as he was going away, he perceived the

coracle covered with skin resting upon the pole of the weir.
Then said one of the weir wards upon Elphin, 'Thou wast never
unlucky until tonight, and now thou hast destroyed the virtues of the weir which always yielded the value of a hundred
pounds every May Eve, and tonight there is nothing but this
skin covered coracle within it.'

"'How now,' said Elphin, 'there may be therein the value
of a hundred pounds.' Well, they took up the coracle, and he
who opened it saw the forehead of the boy and said to Elphin,
'Behold, a radiant brow!' 'Taliesin be he called,' said
Elphin, and he lifted the boy into his arms, and lamenting his
misfortune, he placed him sorrowfully behind him. And he
made his horse canter gently, although before he had been
trotting, and the horses carried him as softly as though he
had been sitting in the easiest chair in the world. Presently
Taliesin made a pronouncement of consolation and praise to
Elphin, and foretold honor to Elphin and the consolation was,
as you may see:

'Fair Elphin, cease to lament!
Let no one be dissatisfifed with his own,
To despair will bring no advantage,
No man sees what supports him;
The prayer of Cynlls will not be in vain;
The Great Spirit will not violate a promise.
Never in Gwuddno's weir
Was there such good luck as this night.
Fair Elphin, dry thy cheeks!
Being too sad will not avail.
Although thou thinkest thou hast no gain,
Too much grief will bring thee no good,
Nor doubt the miracles of the Gods.
Although I am but little, I am highly gifted.
From seas, and from mountains, and
From the depths of rivers,
The Great Spirit brings wealth to the unfortunate man.

Elphin, of lively qualities,
Thy resolution is unmanly;
Thou must not be over-sorrowful:
Better to trust in the Great Spirit than to forebode
    ill.
Weak and small as I am,
On the foaming beach of the ocean,
In the day of trouble I shall be,
Of more service to thee than three
Hundred salmon.
Elphin, of notable qualities, Be
Not displeased at thy misfortune;
Although recline thus weak in my bag,
There lies a virtue in my tongue.
While I continue thy protector
Thou hast not much to fear,
Remembering the names of the Goddess
None shall be able to harm you,'
"And this was the first poem that Taliesin ever sang.
"Thus ended the tale of the Cauldron of Cerridwen."

                    *   *   *   *   *

"Bard, could you explain why this story symbolized
initiation?"

"William, there is much symbolism in this legend. The
year and a day, which has been the traditional probationary
period for novice witches is actually an accurate way of
signifying the actual Solar year in comparison to a Moon year.
Thirteen lunar months of twenty-eight days only comes to
three-hundred sixty four, while three-hundred sixty five is
an actual, or Seasonal Solar year. This necessitates the
addition of one day—the year and a day. It was also a complete cycle of the Sun, therefore symbolic of the rebirth of
the probationer.

"The Cauldron, a female symbol of generation, created the
three mystical drops of Knowledge. This compares with the

                            59

story of Einigan Gawr who saw three rays of light on which were inscribed all knowledge and science. He took three rods of mountain ash, and inscribed all the sciences upon them in imitation of the three rays of light. And those who saw them deified the rods, which so grieved Einigan that he broke the rods and died. After the space of a year and a day, Menw Ab Teirgwaidd saw three rods growing out of the mouth of Einigan, and upon them was every kind of knowledge and science written. Then Menw took the three rods and learned all the sciences, and taught them all except the name of the Great Spirit, from which has originated the Bardic secret, and blessed is he who possesses it.

"By tasting of the three drops of the mystic liquid, Gwion became enlightened and underwent a transformation-- an enlightenment!

"The several shape changes of Gwion are symbols of the several stages in an initiate's enlightenment. Being consumed by Cerridwen and then born of her nine months later is symbolic of the final step of Initiation. The coracle also symbolizes rebirth since Elphin became the foster father of Taliesin, and May Eve is a time of rebirth and Initiation.

"William, does this make any sense at all to you?" she asked somewhat exasperated.

I had been looking up at the clouds but still listening and visualizing. I started, but met her eyes directly.

"Elder, I guess I seem dumb at times but I assure you that I am learning! It's just that these stories aren't like the ones I was used to back in the States, and I have to make a picture in my mind of what is happening."

"William, it will come," she smiled. "Are there any other questions?"

A million buzzing hornets seemed to be in my head, and there were as many questions, but I let the other seekers go first.

60

And afterward, as I thought of all the nursery rhymes and bedtime stories that I had been told as a child I realized that the stories seemed to take on new meanings, although they were still the same stories. Maybe she was right. Maybe all the stories people pass down as folklore, myth, and legend really did contain "secret lore."

As I dropped off to sleep I could taste the three drops.

CHAPTER 5
Eyes of Meditation

CHAPTER FIVE

MEDITATION AND THE CELTIC TREE OF LIFE

"People think that a teacher should perform miracles
and manifest illumination. The requirement in a
teacher, however, is only that he or she should
possess all that a seeker needs." --Rhuddlwm Gawr

Fall was upon us and the fire crackling merrily in
the old stone hearth made us feel warm and cozy. We could
see our breath drift slowly into a musty corner of the house
meeting room as we waited for class. We were growing closer
to one another, and strong feelings of friendship were
developing.

At nine o'clock p.m. we returned to the classroom, where
only a few dark wood desks stood like silent sentinels, and
our guide began again.

"After the Great Destruction of the Third World when
most humans had regressed to a primitive culture, the symbol
of the Tree of Life became a staff struck into the ground,
later a totem pole, and finally, in its simpler form, a
forked stick symbolizing the Horned God. The ancient Celts
regarded the birch as the sacred tree. It was visualized as
the axis of the earth and the summit of the tree was the
North Star.

"The tree passed through nine heavens, each represented
by a step cut into the tree. This symbolism is still used
today in our initiatory process. The Tree of Life is a basic
pattern of consciousness common to all systems of relationship between the inner and the outer world--the search for
Enlightenment.

"What has the Tree of Life to do with meditation? As
the Tree of Life is symbolic of humankind's relationship

63

to the universe, it also is symbolic of humankind's relationship within its own being. As a tree's sap rises in the
Spring when life begins anew, so does the serpent power rise
within an individual as the search for enlightenment begins."

Branwen, one of the older students, noted how much symbolism surrounded this tree.

"It's as if it was a reference point to a significant
area of the Old Religion," she said.

"Yes, that's true," replied the guide. "The study of
the Celtic Tree of Life is cloaked in arcane symbolism. Only
those who have earned the right may be given the keys to the
Tree. Therefore, before any seeker is allowed to attempt the
mastery of the Tree, that individual must first learn the Y
Tylwyth Teg meditation technique."

"Is that any different from other forms?"

"Yes, in many ways. Y Tylwyth Teg meditation is a method
by which the mind can transcend conscious thought."

"But what use is it to Welsh Paganism?" I asked.

"It is one of the basic methods which will open a seeker's
mind to enlightenment. By this method we transcend mind,
thoughts, emotions, and body. We put our innermost self into
intimate contact with the Great Spirit. In this we are sometimes only partially successful since we are only human."

"I've heard of focusing on various points in the body.
Is that important?"

"Yes, there are several spiritiual centers located in the
body: the base of the spine; the genital area; the solar
plexus; the heart area; the thyroid/parathyroid area; the
pituary/thalmus area; and the brain/pineal gland area.   Although these centers are usually dormant in underdeveloped
humans, they may be activated during meditation. These centers influence each and every part of the living human and act
through the ductless glands of the endocrine system.

"These centers react in a different way in each individual,
physically as well as spiritually. Some individuals, because

64

of selfish desires, self-indulgence, and greed have allowed these centers to become atrophied, thereby delaying that individual's chance for advancement."

"What happens during meditation, when the spiritual centers are activated?"

"Meditation releases a creative flow of energy which moves from the base of the spine upward through the body to the pineal gland--the Cauldron of Cerridwen or the Holy Grail of Immortality. It is this cup which overflows into the pituitary gland. Serpent power must be brought into action before one may hope to become enlightened.

"The energy aroused can be used for constructive or destructive purposes, for it knows no morality. Each person has the seeds of good or evil planted within him or her and each is free to choose the pathway to follow.

"Before one attempts to raise this serpent power in meditation, it is necessary that the physical body be properly prepared. Without this preparation, one may become influenced by outside forces, for all desires and powers become accentuated. As each spiritual center becomes activated, its memory pattern becomes reawakened and aspects of karma, talents, and abilities become noticeable to the individual."

"How will we notice it?"

"The base of the spine is the area where the serpent power is generated. This is the source of the creative force of life. There, the power lies coiled up like a serpent, three and a half times. When this force awakens and begins to move up the spine step by step, the person begins to unfold and a great gift is left at each spiritual center."

"Will it cause physical changes?"

"From the beginning the power moves up through the neurohormonal spiritual centers mentioned before, the ductless glands. These glands govern the body's growth, metabolism, sexual activity, etc., and are controlled by the mind. Since these glands are affected by our thought patterns, it is conceivable that most of the medical problems plaguing humankind

65

could be alleviated by the harmonious function of these
glands. Meditation can repair those glands which are mal-
functioning and causing problems."

"Which glands will be affected?"

"In males these are the testicles which generate sperm
cells, in women these are the ovaries which secrete the
egg cells which must be fertilized by the sperm before conception takes place. Other hormones are secreted by these
glands which affect one's emotional, spiritual, and mental
health. Other sexual glands are the prostrate gland in males
and the cells of leydig which secrete endrogen. For this
reason, balanced sexuality is needed in each individual.

"The solar plexus center is more neurological because
of the mass of nerve ganglion located there. Also, several
important glands are located here. These are the pancreas
and the adrenals. The pancreas generates insulin and
digestive fluids and regulates our blood sugar balance.

"The adrenal glands perched on top of the kidneys produce
adrenalin, cortin, and over forty other hormones. Adrenalin
is the fight or flight hormone. It can give one superhuman
strength if enough is produced. Cortin regulates sexual
maturity and function. It is in the cells of the adrenals
that the karmic patterns are carried from one lifetime to
another.

"Within the heart area is a mystery gland called the
thymus, which governs certain stages of development in children
prior to puberty. It begins to shrink and atrophy after the
ovaries and gonads begin to function. This is the seat of
the personality and the seat of the lower self. The thymus
gland represents the evolving principle of mankind. This
influence can work for good or evil in an individual. The
four lower centers represent the material or physical part of
humankind that one must strive to master if one is to become
fully enlightened.

66

"The three upper centers are the thyroid/parathyroid, the pineal and the pituitary. The thyroid and the parathyroid are two sets of glands on both sides of the throat. They are responsible for our basic metabolism. The parathyroid regulates the calcium balance in our bodies. This center is also related to the willpower of an individual.

"The pineal gland is the seat of the soul memory. It is located in the middle of the brain, about the size of a pea. Its function is to produce a hormone which, when secreted into the brain, throws a person into a deep mystical experience. When this center is opened, the individual will receive a spiritual name and can recall to memory all that the soul has been since it was created.

"The serpent energy spills over into the pituitary gland from the pineal gland. This is the master gland. It is located at the front underside of the brain. It is the healing center of the body and expresses the universal love.

"Different mystical traditions have different placements for the third eye. Some place it in association with the pineal gland which is made up of both nerve cells and gland cells, and in certain reptiles is highly developed. This gland, which is located in the middle of the brain could conceivably at one time have been a gland which regulated the functions of the body in relation to the sun, since a pigmentation hormone is also found within it. The pituitary gland, which is located at the base of the brain, is also associated with optic nerves as well as tactile nerves. The more we discover about the human body and the endocrine system, the more we find that there is a harmonious relation between the endocrine glands and the central nervous sytem, as well as outside forces."

I was beginning to wonder if I would personally experience all this. My body for the most part was still very much on a normal course.

"Do we all react the same," I asked, "or do some of us advance faster than other? If so, is there a way to speed up this sense of bodily harmony with outside forces?"

"Each individual reacts to different stimuli in different ways. One person may react to Tibetan chimes while others may not react at all. Music is quite helpful as a stimulus, for all meditation stimulus seems to have a vibratory source. For instance, mantras are sounds which initiate the sacred vibration rate when uttered by an individual while meditating."

"What about different positions of the body?"

"Above all, your back needs to be straight at all times. This allows the serpent power to flow easily and at a constant rate."

"What other mystical influences are there?"

"One of the oldest is fragrance or odor. Nothing is odorless. Each of us exudes our own individual scent which dogs, cats, other animals, and people with a keen sense of smell can immediately recognize. Many factors determine the intensity and type of color that exudes from us: our state of health; thought patterns; and spiritual advancement.

"Odor is the oldest means of influencing peoples' two deepest instincts: sex and religion. Knowing the secret power of perfumes, the priests and priestesses of Y Tylwyth Teg and before them the priests and priestesses of ancient civilizations mixed compounds of precious ointments so powerful that the fragrances of some have endured for thousands of years. Sealed vases of alabaster found in tombs of Egyptian pharohs and recently opened, have yielded the aromas of balsam and myrrh.

"The primary aim of our use of fragrances is to stimulate the base of the spine spiritual center, thereby releasing the serpent power. In general, the scents used for these purposes are oil of jasmine for the hands, patchouli for the cheeks and breasts, spikenard for the hair, musk for the mons veneria, sandalwood for the thighs, and saffron for the feet."

I was off on a mental tangent again, drifting with the
silken vapors--rich oriental fragrances misting on my cheeks,
nourishing them with the subtle odors released from imagined
jars as though the eastern kings had appeared through our
heavily latched wood door. I aroused, sharply trembling
with illusions of medieval visions.

My senses rushed on with heightened awareness and hunger.
The wind direction shifted. From the subtle nuances of
odors--light airs on a new sail--the steadier proclamation
of north-westerlies arrived. Now this I was more familiar
with. The gusts and storm patterns, ravishing hunger, the
extremes--tornado winds gulping up everything in sight, then
spitting it all out in harsh whirling mischief. I sensed
my body trying to pull all this knowledge together into
some inner logic--a sensitive, yet steady breeze--the odor of
perfume--a balance.

"There are two ways of obtaining physical balance for
Y Tylwyth Teg meditation techniques: diet and exercise."

My body began to soak in slowly the wholeness of the
suggested foods, as though the words themselves brought food
and nutrition into my parched skin.

"The Y Tylwyth Teg diet seeks to cleanse the mind and
spirit through the use of natural whole grain products such
as wheat, barley, buckwheat, and small grains; leafy green
vegetables; potatoes and other root vegetables; peas and
beans; fresh milk and buttermilk; clarified butter and cheese;
eggs; sun dried and fresh fruit and rarely lean meat; grape
wine; and fish.

"The bread must be wholesome, unrefined and preferably
stoneground. It is important that the bran and the germ
kernal be kept a part of the final product. The bran is the
outer covering and is important in the digestive process.
The germ kernel contains vitamin E, essential in strengthening the reproductive system, the glandular system, the heart
and general muscular system, and the nervous system.

69

"By some, milk is considered a complete food, but that
is only if the milk is unprocessed. If it is pasteurized
it is almost worthless. The cream must be separated from
the milk, and from this butter and cottage cheese are made.
Buttermilk, a by-product of butter-making, is an excellent,
nutritious drink. Yogurt, a product of bacterial action, is
also an excellent food.

"Vegetables and greens are also a very important part
of the diet. They are for the most part eaten raw: spinach,
lettuce, cabbage, peas, turnips, squash, potatoes, onions,
bean sprouts, and herbs. Herbs are used in cooking, in
salads, and in herbal teas and medicines. All vegetables
should be organic and natural.

"A little meat may be also eaten, but certain types are
more important than others, liver and lean meat among them.

"Fruits are also essential: apricots, peaches, cherries,
apples, pears, grapes, pineapples, lemons, oranges, etc.

"Wine from grapes, naturally fermented, is both a delight
to the palatte and a source of essential minerals and other
elements.

"The following minerals are very important to the diet:
*Calcium rich foods, eaten with fruit.
*Phosphorus, contained in whole grains and dairy products
   as well as eggs, meats, and nuts.
*Spinach, taken with vinegar, for iron.
*Iodine, probably one of the most important minerals,
   needed by the thyroid gland for correct operation, can
   be found in cod liver oil, kelp, raw sea salt, and fish.
*Copper, which is necessary for the proper utilization
   of iron, also prevents anemia. The best sources are
   sea food, liver, molasses, green leafy vegetables, and
   soy products.
*Sodium, which is necessary to keep calcium in solution
   and the body in an acid-alkaline balance. Sodium can
   be found in sea salt.

70

*Potassium is important for body growth and functions
as a balance. Dark molasses, kelp, leafy green vegetables, and fruit are excellent sources.

*Magnesium is necessary to maintain mineral balance in
the body and elasticity of the muscles. Chlorophyll
is a good source, as well as cereal grains.

*Manganese gives strength to tissues and bones. Green
leaves and whole grains contain considerable amounts
of manganese.

*Chlorine is a part of the gastric juices as an acid.
Sodium chloride, again, is an excellent source.

*Carbon, hydrogen, oxygen, and nitrogen are the building
blocks of the human body and are obtained from carbohydrates.

*And cobalt is essential in the production of red cor-
puscles and glandular activity."

Listening to the recital of nourishing foods, I had sub-
consciously begun a slow rhythmic breathing process until I
had recovered a sense of calm and felt my body taking in with
ease the knowlege of these rich nutrients. I tried to recall
how long it had been a habit to eat the heavy fried foods
which I had enjoyed since my youth. I shook off a sensation
of discomfort and breathed slowly out as the discussion continued, expanding to include knowledge of enzymes and special
foods such as honey, yogurt, and wheat germ.

"Raw liver and sun-ripened fruits are excellent sources
of enzymes. Nuts, also, such as almonds, coconuts, pecans,
walnuts, beechnuts, hazelnuts, peanuts, etc., are essential
for a complte diet. Papayas, rich in Vitamins A and C, are
rich in digestive enzymes.

"Lecithin enhances fat metabolism and is found in soy-
bean oil.

"Wheat germ and wheat germ oil are rich sources of B and
E vitamins. They also contain valuable proteins and fats.

71

"Include honey in your daily diet. Look for a dark colour, and naturally unheated and unstrained. It has a high sugar content--dextrose, sucrose, glucose, and levulose. Honey also contains an abundant supply of minerals and vitamins, among them are Vitamin C, thiamin, riboflavin, and other members of the B complex group.

"Yogurt, kefir, and other types of cultured milk supply valuable acids which assist digestion and are beneficial for the friendly bacteria in the digestive tract.

"Brewer's yeast is an excellent source of protein and B vitamin complex."

I was particularly fascinated with our guide's teachings on fasting. I held vague contradictory beliefs about the mystics who dreamed in emaciated bodies and entered a sort of celestial high after weeks of fasting. Again there was a spiritual/physical logic surrounding these teachings that added to my sense of calm. And always the concepts of balance, natural rhythms, and time cycles were revealed.

"Fasting is rebirth--rebirth through the flushing out of waste material from the system. Fasting not at just anytime either, but tuned into the body's rhythms at the height of the biorhythmic cycle. Fasting at least once a month for two or three days, the rhythm is maintained with a longer period of sustained fasting to be tried once a year for up to ten days during the springtime season.

"You have poisoned yourself. Civilization will not die by the sword; it will crumble by virtue of its disintegrating stomach.

"All life on this planet is being permeated with all manner of insecticides, pesticides, fertilizers, antibiotics, hormones, enzymes, drugs, poisonous elements such as mercury, cadmium, and arsenic, and DDT just to mention a few.

"Artificial colors, artificial preservatives, artificial food--they are part of your life.

"Humankind takes a beautiful food such as whole grain wheat and destroys its food value. First, the bran is removed which would aid digestion and contribute enzymes and vitamins to the diet. Then the germ is removed which contains most of the protein and enzymes, leaving the carbohydrate--starch--which your bakeries make bread from.

"William, a developing human needs a well balanced diet in order for the mind to function properly. Every day, you must see that you obtain the proper amount of water, minerals, vitamins, carbohydrates, fats, and protein. If these components are obtained in the improper amount, your system will be imbalanced."

"But what if I can't find decent food around the area I will be living in?" I asked.

"William, how important is your body to you? Don't try to fool me. That question was a cop-out! You can always find sources of good food wherever you are, even if you have to grow it yourself or move closer to a good supply.

"Remember, eating is one of the actions that attaches us to the Earth, for everything we eat is like consuming part of the Earth. Eating, therefore, is a sacrament. If you do not consume good quality food because of contaminants you are negating its spiritual value. Most humans, by eating at quick-food restaurants and eating food canned, or worse, synthetically produced, are robbing themselves of the basic life giving elements of the Earth.

"Hypocrites said, 'When someone has fallen ill, he should change his way of living. It is clear that his way of life is bad, wholly or to a large extent, or in some way.' Those words are still relevant today.

"William, diseases have various causes, some related and some not. Every disease known to man is caused because the body's defense mechanism broke down. If the diet is deficient in a specific element such as a mineral or a vitamin, a specific disease will result. This is because in order to operate

73

normally the body needs that mineral or vitamin. If it does
not receive it in the food we eat or cannot manufacture it,
the body will soon begin to degenerate.

"For instance, total lack of Vitamin C will cause a
condition known as scurvy which can eventually cause death.
But even if there is only a deficiency the body will still
suffer by being prone to infection.

"Without iodine in the diet our thyroid would soon cease
functioning, which would keep us from metabolizing our food
and effectively starving us to death.

"You see, each vitamin and each mineral has a place in
the matrix of life and without any one of them the others
would soon be useless, because the body would die."

"But Sarah, if civilization keeps poisoning our food,
won't we all end up dying anyway?"

"Yes, and the point of no return is rapidly approaching."

"That's terrifying!" I exclaimed.

"Yes, it is, but there is hope on two accounts."

"What are they?"

"The first is that Humanity may finally wake up before
it is too late. This is not likely, however."

"What is the second?"

"That nature, pushed into a state of imbalance by
Humanity will compensate. Remember, the Earth is a living
thing. By introducing various toxins into the environment we
will cause certain reactions to occur in the Earth, preventing
our further interference.

"William, by now you must have realized that every species,
every variety of life was created for a purpose, and each
species of life performs a function on this Earth. They can't
help it--their instincts demand it. It seems that only Humanity has the power to ignore instinctual patterning and
cause disharmony.

"If you leave here with nothing else, take this knowlege
with you: It is not the purpose of humankind to change nature

74

to suit itself. It is the purpose of humankind to change
nature to suit itself. It is the purpose of humankind to
live in harmony with nature, using its reasoning power to
protect nature from outside forces. Think of Humanity as a
super antibody in the giant living body of the Earth.

"If we control our growth and only respond to attacks
on the Earth by external forces, we are performing our function well and the Earth is healthy. But if we grow uncon-
trollably, destroying the Earth in the process, we are like
a cancer which grows by consuming its host."

After class, I walked out on the heath and stood silently
looking out over the hills, thinking of wheels within wheels,
ideas within ideas--What does it all mean?

I looked up at the stars. It was a clear night and
I could see thousands of bright pinpoints of light. If we
are living beings, living as parasites on the Earth, and the
Earth is a living thing revolving around the living sun, and
the living solar system revolves around the living milky
way galaxy, and there are an infinite number of galaxies,
then there is no end to creation.

Then what is our purpose? Why am I here?

Something began to open up within me. Something stirred.

"You think, therefore you are," something said. "You
exist, you feel, and you are part of the whole. The Great
Spirit is the universe and you are part of the universe."

"But what is my purpose?" I asked in frustration.

"Your purpose is to live out your life as a human being,
walking in balance with Nature and constrained only by your
love of life. Life is sacred. This does not mean that death
is unnatural, it only means that every living thing was
created for a purpose. After that purpose is fulfilled that
entity may go back to the astral plane. The universe is a
school. We are the students and the teachers. Our paths
lead to the Great Spirit, for as we walk in understanding
of the pattern of life, we come closer and closer to the Great
Spirit.

"The only truth is that this physical plane we experience is an illusion. Things are not what they seem. Listen to the still small voice within you; for only there will you find the answer."

How frustrating to always receive only half the answer. But this something that was talking to me was myself, so it was understandable.

Suddenly, I realized that I was listening only to the wind and I was awakening from some sort of half sleep. Even though I still had not found the Grail, I was closer.

The rhythm of Life, Death, and Rebirth through the body-mind-spirit was beginning to trace itself within the cords, fibers, and invisible patterns of my being. I was ready for the next teaching--the first meditation technique.

Sarah was speaking.

"Lie down in a comfortable position, arms at the sides with palms up. Your feet should be about six inches apart. Before we relax our minds we must learn to relax our bodies. Do not hurry. Take your time."

I felt a little tense.

"First, close your eyes. We do not want distractions. Then roll your head back and forth and find a comfortable position for it."

Our guide led us easily into this spiritual exercise which would cause such deeply felt changes in our beings and bring us down to new depths of feeling and understanding.

"Take a couple of deep breaths. Now, keeping your body still, focus your mind on your feet. Feel your toes, your nails, your skin. Explore the muscles and bones. Command your feet over and over to relax and say to yourself, 'I am relaxing my feet. I am relaxing my feet.' Relax-relax-relax."

H-m-m-m, this felt good!

"Next, focus your mind on your ankles. Explore and feel them. You don't have to visualize them, just feel them. Now send the suggestion, 'I am relaxing my ankles, relax-relax-relax,' over and over. Don't hurry."

My ankles felt like rubber.

"Next, focus your mind on your legs from your ankles to your knees. Send the suggestion, 'Relax-relax-relax-I am relaxing my legs.' Explore your calf, your skin, the shin, and the bones.

"Now, focus your mind on your knees. Explore and feel them. Relax them as you did your legs."

I felt a twing in my funny bone.

"Focus your mind on your thighs. Explore and feel them, and relax them.

"Now focus your attention on your rectum and visualize liquid gold light flowing into it. Explore the rectum--the anus. You males, relax the prostrate glands. Just give them the command to relax.

"Next focus your mind on your ovaries or testicles. Relax them and fill them with liquid golden light. Include the whole reproductive system. Explore and feel this entire area.

"Now focus your mind on your lower abdomen. Relax and explore this area completely.

"Relax and explore your lower back. See if you can explore your spine, your sides and continuously relax this area.

"Focus your mind on your stomach and bowels. This is the pancreas area. Fill it with liquid golden light and relax it. Now explore the rest of the interior. Relax it completely.

"Now put your attention on your mid-back and relax it. Visualize your kidneys and relax your adrenal glands located on top of each kidney. Fill each adrenal gland with liquid golden light and relax them."

I felt energy rise up my spinal cord. My back began to tremble.

"Explore and relax your breast area. If you are a woman trace the shape of your breast. If you are a man feel the hair on your chest.

77

"Now find the thymus, which is located near your heart. Fill it with liquid golden light and relax it.

"Locate your heart. Give your heart the suggestion to relax while exploring it. Relax your lungs, your spine.

"Now relax your shoulder blades, your shoulders, your hands, your wrists, your arms, and elbows and throat. Focus your mind on your thyroid/parathyroid glands and fill them with liquid golden light and relax them.

"Relax your face, your cheeks, your chin, your lips, your tongue, your teeth and gums, your eyes, ears, forehead, scalp, your brain. Fill your entire brain with liquid golden light, focusing your mind on the pineal and pituitary glands. Tell them to relax.

"Now watch your breath for approximately three minutes. Just feel the breath flowing and do not try to control it. As you breathe in, mentally say 'Rama.' As you breathe out say 'Tho.'"

For the next few minutes we watched our breath and said our mantras. After ten minutes we were told to become aware and move our arms.

In this first period of reawakening, realigning with the stepped up pace of normal thinking, I began to realize that I had experienced a new sensation of time, and that perhaps an unmistakeable link to other frames of awareness had been made. I was conscious of an altered course or pathway of thinking and feeling, and I joyfully bathed in a sense of time that could last forever.

But we were nearing the end of our temporal visit with this other 'world of time.' How tempting to let this go on and on.

Moving our arms to the light rhythm of the day's rain as though swimming to the surface of a comfortable pool, we heard our guide's further instructions.

"Go on and repeat this meditation technique each day until a new one is taught. Practice meditation diligently, my children, for continuity is most important."

78

She encouraged us to choose an hour of the day or night when we would be most totally ready to devote our minds and bodies to this one purpose. But she cautioned that meditation is not sleep and should be done when our minds and bodies are alert.

Her enthusiasm was gentle and it was also broad and joyful. She was alert with deep green vibrant eyes that told us how wonderful the experiences of meditation could be.

"Never a chore--no, meditation should not be like that-- not like a chore."

She seemed to underline her positive feelings for the value of this experience with gentle insistence.

"Keep trying. You'll get it. Keep trying.

"Each individual is a part of the universe and must be able to comprehend it as an integral facet of the Great Spirit. Each person affects every other person and must be willing to help others if enlightenment is to be attained."

At this point we were opening up to a new level of mystic awareness. But she cautioned:

"If all instructions are followed correctly, the seeker will eventually open up the seven spiritual centers. But, remember our discussion of the Celtic Tree at the beginning of this chapter? There were nine steps cut in the birch tree. We have attained seven of them. The remaining two are the God and Goddess of nature--the Lady and Her Consort. Only by mystic exercises may these steps be reached.

"In many important ways the Y Tylwyth Teg meditation technique is a secret doctrine imparted only by word of mouth from guide to seeker. Even the writings available to us in our thirteen books are intelligible only to those who hold the key to their symbolism and inner meaning."

I sensed that I had committed myself to obtain the key. It was a poignant feeling, and I shivered in expectation of accomplishing my goal--finding my self.

HOD

JESOD

CHAPTER 6
Physical Exercise through the Path

CHAPTER SIX

THE MYSTIC EXERCISES

"Expect nothing--take away experiences, including
the negative ones, as merely steps on the path,
and proceed." --Rhuddlwm Gawr

Frequently, after a period of intensive teaching, I
would find myself wandering out alone on the hills, sorting
out the days and the experiences; absorbing the philosophy,
pulling together the legends, the rituals and the contradic-
tions of my own life.

The hard work of the fall harvesting had brought sore-
ness to my body at times but generally a feeling of well
being too. Now, I felt exhilarated by the fresh air and
cool sunny afternoon walk in the hills, the rich treasures
of fall before the deep cold of winter set in.

After several miles, I found an outcropping of rocks,
gray-green lichens etched in their sides, and sat down.

A few dry weeds grew at the base of the rocks. I broke
off some stalks and thought about the dryness, the brittle-
ness of my own bones and spirit before coming to this place.
I was beginning to feel the effects of the mystic exercises.
It seemed that they allowed for the more complex teaching
to sink in. The exercises are not just another series of
calisthenics or football-type warm ups. They involved an
internal energy flow, after slow and graceful strengthening
of my inner organs and inner will. Even the harshness of
the hills had diminished as the effects of the rhythmic
breathing and fluid body movements took over and replaced
my old style of jerky walking and pounding a path with
aggressive lungs and a sense of urgency.

These new exercises, part of an ancient training system
that was used long before Atlantis sank beneath the waves,

Purification bath

were inspiring a sense of awe in me. The ancients knew how, through certain exercises, to put oneself in contact with one's own inner life force; to manipulate this vital force that stirs within each of us, and to move this energy around the body. Even now, advanced Elders often direct energy to flow into their hands in order to heal themselves and others.

The fibers of my body were beginning to respond as though affected physically by the music of a wooden flute, its harmonious tones drifting through the craggy hills and echoing in the valley.

We were now following the rituals and directions of the ancients, setting aside a period of time in the morning and just before the evening meal to make the exercise part of the rhythm of the day--as natural as sleeping or eating.

Each morning we would go to our "place of peace" singled out by each of us as conducive to concentration--a place of calm and peaceful energy fields. This was important so that concentration could reach a peak.

Fresh air was also important because deep breathing is a crucial element in the exercises and is the source of vital energy.

This "place of peace" also encouraged peaceful, non-destructive thoughts and combined the forces of mind, spirit, and physical beings into a single channel, concentrating the energy into a new alignment of healthy power and physical strength.

Meditation was a very important preliminary to freeing our minds, and we began our exercises after periods of medi-tation.

We were admonished to stop smoking entirely and refrain from drinking more than three glasses of wine a day. Smoking is obviously harmful because it prevents the development of deep lung power necessary to the success of the exercises, meditation, and health.

As the sun disappeared behind a mass of clouds looming over the distant horizon and the mountains cooled to gray-gold shadows, I started back down the rocky path.

The path led toward a simple cottage almost hidden behind a stone wall draped with ivy. As I approached the gate, a sheep dog barked happily and trotted up the path toward me. The simplicity of the place encouraged me to linger and visit awhile.

One of the elders, an old gentleman of gentle manners, was walking in the garden and looked up as I opened the gate and entered the yard.

This setting contrasted sharply with the uneasy, yet stimulating days preceeding my journey to Wales.

Sarah had warned me in London that things would not be peaches and cream when I got here. The morning we left she insisted that I be very sure of my decision because there would be a great deal of work and dedication involved. She was right. I had literally been working my ass off since I arrived.

By now the Elder had returned to the cottage and emerged carrying a pot of tea and some biscuits. As was the custom, I waited until he acknowledged my presence before I approached the table set up by the solitary tree.

His weathered face and clear blue eyes seemed to encourage a feeling of security as he waved me over.

"C'mon lad, have a cup of tea."

I sat down in the offered chair and gratefully accepted his hospitality.

"You've been up in the hills quite a while, haven't you? I saw you pass through the upper meadow this morning."

I nodded as I enjoyed the last of the afternoon sun with him and one of the finest cups of tea I had ever tasted--sweet, rich, and aromatic. He had a few tales to share with me, but my mind drifted off as I listened.

84

The cup of tea had warmed my body and as I bit on a few stray tea leaves I thought of how I was refining my dietary habits, cutting down on meat and eating more natural whole grains and fresh vegetables.

I had discovered that the most important aspect of exercise was the preliminary preparation--the move toward relaxation, the reduction of tension.

After I learned to relax my body, I worked on developing my deep breathng techniques which increased my concentration ability. I was also developing grace in my movements as I floated gently from one position to another with a soft, ballet-like quality.

My mind woke from its lethargy as the Elder cleared the table and wished me a pleasant afternoon. He returned to his garden, and I returned to the path.

The next day Sarah came with me up to the hills. We walked with exuberance up through several valleys of ferns, past the grazing sheep in the upper pastures, to a rolling plateau with rocky cliffs and hidden caves, above the world.

We began our exercises and pulled our relaxed muscles into lithe, flexible cords, like free-flowing vines hanging from large trees. I felt a sense of joy in the movements and I discovered that the tight knots were disappearing more and more each day, yielding to new lines of energy.

Sarah began to speak, her voice moving into sonorous tones that matched the smooth, slate-green of the rocks.

"Let's warm up, William."

I moved my body automatically into position, stationing my feet apart approximately the width of my shoulders, relaxing my arms and hands.

"Let your arms dangle loosely now, William, and shake all the tension out."

I kicked a few stones away from the grassy area, feeling the energy begin to flow, and felt the same sensations as I shook my right and then left legs.

85

"How is your neck, William?'

"Fine except for a couple of kinks." I had injured my
neck when I was a child and it had always bothered me.

I relaxed my neck muscles and let my head drop forward,
then slowly revolved it clockwise twice as I'd learned and
reversed to a counter-clockwise turn.

A loud crack of my upper spine had us both laughing.

"You're getting so good at relaxing, you're going to
start a rock slide!"

I looked back up over my shoulder teasingly and cringed,
as though a few boulders were on their way down.

"Okay, where were we?"

"Bring your hands up from your sides, your palms parallel
to the ground. Move slowly, William, and hold your arms in
front of your body. Continue on up until your arms are
stretched overhead."

I reached high, feeling my body open up as the energy
followed my breathing. At the same time, I raised myself
high on the balls of my feet. I counted to five, holding
the position, and then sank back on my heels as my arms
flowed slowly back to my sides.

"Let's try it a couple more times."

I followed her lead and then as we took a break, I leaned
back against a boulder to watch the clouds rolling in,
drinking in the fresh mountain air.

Sarah smiled her enormously charming smile and then, like
a drill sergeant, had me concentrating again on a new exercise.

"Concentrate on a point just below your navel, William,
and stand straighter." She looked over my position and corrected it.

I worked myself into a relaxed, concentrated stance with
feet slightly apart, hands open and held loosely at my sides.
I kept my toes stationary and forced · my heels outward as
she had instructed me. At the same time, I made my hands
into a fist and swung them to the front of my body at waist
level. She eyed my movements approval and smiled.

"Now keep your heels stationary and simultaneously force your toes outward as you pull your fists back to your sides."

"Are you sure I'm not supposed to chant something and roll my stomach simultaneously?" I asked with a sarcastic grin.

"C'mon now. You're not concentrating! You're waggling around like a sheep dog."

"A sheep dog! Me?"

"Concentrate, William. We're trying to make this part flow smoother. Keep your toes stationary and move your heels out again while bringing your fists in front of your waist. Then swing your toes out—your heels still solidly fixed—until your feet are parallel with each other. Now plant your fists firmly on your thighs."

As I finished the last movement, she said, "Now start over. Repeat the movements until they flow smoothly."

After about five minutes I seemed to have mastered it.

"Now, draw back your arms and keep your fists facing forward. At the same time, keeping your back as straight as possible, bend your knees slightly . . . Good! But, remember, the knees should never tilt forward more than one-half the length of your foot."

I moved my knee back slightly.

"Your head, neck, and back must form a straight line even with the back of your feet. This is called the position of the horse since it resembles an individual riding a horse. Now consciously begin the deep breathing exercises."

I exhaled deeply through my nose, while I expanded my abdomen without moving my chest. Using my diaphragm as I exhaled, I followed the stream down my throat into the top of my lungs, down through the middle lung and into my lower lung. I let my lungs fill slowly from the bottom up. As I exhaled, I placed my tongue at the roof of my mouth and blew the air out through my teeth. I began to feel something stirring at the base of my spine!

87

"Good, William! That was very smooth. Now use your imagination. Channel your breath through your body from the back of your head to the base of your spine, then up the front of your body and out your mouth. Continue deep breathing for as long as you can hold the horse position."

With the warm up exercises over, I was inclined to play sheep dog again, but a glance at the sky caused me to note a changing look to the clouds. They were sweeping in on us, causing slate-blue shadows on the surrounding hills. Sarah's eyes were sober, blue and intent. They seemed to swallow up the mountains, hills, shadows, me--everything.

Her energy focused mine. So, we began the first exercise. We laid down on the meadow grass, relaxing completely, and I let loose from my mind all cares, worries, and thoughts. I expelled all air from my lungs by quietly drawing in my abdomen as I exhaled. I slowly refilled my lungs, Sarah counting to seven as my mind echoed her soft voice.

We repeated this twelve times, then inhaled through both nostrils and filled our lungs as full as possible. I held my breath in my mouth with a new level of concentration I hadn't experienced before, then using my abdominal muscles I forced all the air out of my lungs.

As we repeated this exercise, we now recited the words, "Ram-a" while inhaling.

"Picture a glowing cosmic force flowing into your lungs. Envision this vital stream flowing through all the psychic channels of your astral body and then into your physical body, energizing each cell," Sarah gently suggested.

After the exercise, as we walked down the pathway toward the community, Sarah reminded me that I was to work on the breathing exercises twelve times a day.

Up here in the hills you feel so full and rich, the air makes you feel like flying! I had a week to master the breathing exercises until I became able to move smoothly and rhythmically. This gave me a sensation of lifting my entire body off the ground--like floating on a cloud.

88

By the next week, the process of meditation, breathing, concentration, and movement of body was developing into a unified experience. Again, Sarah and I sought the calm of the hills to practice.

We had spent the morning scrambling over the boulders, slipping through the clefts and up the steep slopes, then wandering lazily over the meadows toward a far slope, burnished with coppery shadows on the light stand of wildflowers and tufts of meadow grass. The sun never fully burned through the low mist as we practiced. Relaxing our bodies, we inhaled slowly through the nose, inflating first the lower, middle, and finally upper areas of our lungs. I began drifting off, easily floating now, when Sarah pulled me back gently as if she had a silk rope.

"Time yourself with your pulse, William. Breathe in, filling your lungs completely by the count of four pulse beats. Hold your breath for a count of two, then exhale for four, deflating your lungs from the top to the bottom. Hold your breath for a count of two and then repeat twelve times."

This was to be done twelve times a day for a week.

As the week continued and it became colder, rain splattered on our windows and created great waterfalls off the roof. Sea-bearing winds roared up the slopes toward our upland valley, ending for a time the Fall hikes, pulling us into our sweaters and woolen slacks like turtles. New exercises and new instructions were showed with a certain shivering eagerness, but in the quiet privacy of our cold rooms, it took more discipline than the relaxed openness of the hills to endure. Still, the concentration allowed us to enter our minds through a gate of higher awareness.

Sitting at night in my room, softly lit with a single oil lamp, I began the third set of breathing exercises. First, I cleaned all air from my lungs, exhaling forcefully.

Then, closing the right nostril with the right thumb, I slowly
inhaled through the left nostril to the count of four pulse
beats. I then closed both nostrils and retained my breath
for a count of sixteen. Keeping the left nostril closed,
I exhaled through my right nostril for a count of eight,
then with my left nostril still closed, I inhaled through my
right nostril for a count of four and again held my breath
for a count of sixteen.

The rain pounded on the windows and threatened to interrupt my concentration, but I had become stronger mentally
and pulled my mind and body into full unity.

Closing my right nostril, I exhaled through my left
nostril for eight beats. I then repeated this sequence four
more times and meditated for a half an hour.

By the fourth week, I noticed a perceptible difference
in my appearance as I shaved in the morning. I saw the same
flesh, beard, dark, hazel eyes which seemed to change to blue
at times, though never too intense. My face was slightly
thinner but the few lines seemed to have softened which
surprised me. In fact, my face appeared to be less rugged
yet without weak lines. Even my hair, usually a dark blonde
in winter, had soft light tones in it, in contrast to the
heavy sun bleaching it had acquired at the Mediterranean.

*   *   *   *   *

I was into a new set of exercises that were pinned to
my bedroom wall on a piece of wrapping paper.

"Sitting very straight, take a few complete breaths.
Now inhale one last time. Don't move your chest or shoulders.
Breathe with your diaphragm. Now contract the abdominal
muscles, exhaling suddenly and forcefully. Allow the bottom
of the lungs to inflate again. Blast the air out by the
forceful contractions of your abdominal muscles. Continue
this for sixty times.

"Begin at a very slow pace and speed it up as the exercise goes on. After finishing sixty, do several complete

breaths. Hold the last breath for sixty seconds. Repeat the above exercises three times."

I was very aware of the energy level increasing in my body as I completed the third series of sixty breaths.

"After completion of the breathing exercise continue with the following:

"Stand erect, spine straight, feet comfortably apart with your hands relaxed at your sides.

"Inhaling, turn your palms out and slowly bring them over your head, inscribing a circle in the air with both arms. By the end of the inhalation your hands should be directly over your head and your fingers interlocked.

"Holding your breath for a moment, turn your palms outward and then over so that they are now facing the sky, whereas they previously faced your head.

"Exhaling slowly, push your hands and entire body skyward until you are on the balls of your feet. Still exhaling, lower yourself until your feet are back on the floor and your hands are just over your head.

"Again, hold your breath for a moment, and flip your palms over so that they are facing your head. Inhaling, unlock your fingers and slowly let your arms drop to your sides, forming a semi-circle in much the same way you did earlier in the exercise."

I was to do the exercise four times the first month and six times the third month.

"The second exercise is as follows:

"Inhaling, jump into the horse position and hold this position until your lungs are completely filled.

"Turning your head to the right, bring your left arm across your chest and hold it in a claw shape just as if you are clutching the strings of a bow. Bring the right hand up to chest height with the index finger and thumb extended upward and the remaining three fingers bent. This is crucial. The fingers in this position become the focal point for your body's energy.

91

"As a beginner, you will experience very discernable energy sensations during the rest of these movements when the fingers are extended in this position."

I could feel the energy flowing through channels in my body--in through my mouth, down to the base of my spine, and back up to the front of my body.

"The claw position of the left hand, which imitates the way a bowstring is drawn, maximizes the effectiveness of the movement by providing a counter exertion in the opposite direction.

"When the hands have reached the position, your lungs should be completely filled. Exhale as you gradually push your right hand out to shoulder height, and pull your left hand back, almost as if you were pulling a real bowstring taunt.

"After the maximum stretch point is reached, relax the bow while exhaling completely.

"Your hands now gradually dissolve the bow structure. As the bow dissolves, both hands pass in front of the chest and begin a new cycle.

"Still inhaling, reform the bow on your left side with your right hand in the claw shape and the left as the energy focal point. Exhaling, pull the bow taunt, as it was earlier on the right side of your body. Still exhaling, relax the bow, return the hands to the horse position, and take a deep breath before going on and repeating the exercise."

At the end of the third month we learned more advanced mystic exercises. It was during the fourth month that I was named!

CHAPTER 7
"Alone on the Mountainside"

CHAPTER SEVEN

INITIATION

"Do not follow the footsteps of the old ones--Seek
what they sought." --Rhuddlwm Gawr

I had just awakened from a deep sleep by the wind when
I heard the first "Ha-Hooooo!" I had been in this shallow
cave for seven days now witout food, melting snow for my
water because I had stupidly knocked over the water jug in
my sleep the second night. I had a sleeping bag, a blanket,
and tools to build a fire, but every morning found me with
cold feet and a fire to start anew.

"Ha-Hooooo!" I yelled back. Now the Elder knew I was
still alive and I could have the rest of the day to myself.
Funny, I wasn't giddy anymore, just a little weak but clearheaded with a strange feeling of euphoria at times. The wind
was still blowing around noon when I went out on the side of
the mountain to find wood. I found something else too--
the second step to enlightenment.

I had gotten an armload of sticks, bark and branches
and was making my way back to the cave when all at once there
seemed to be someone in front of me. I blinked and even
though the figure seemed to drift in and out of focus as
if in a movie, it still looked just like a real person.

"Excuse me, sir," I said, raising my voice above the
wind. "I didn't see you. I shouldn't even be talking to
you. I am supposed to avoid all persons."

He pointed down at my feet and I suddenly realized I was
floating about six inches above the rocky path!

I was startled and confused, curious all at once.
Breathing, not breathing. Blinking, not blinking. Numb,
serene. It all seemed to fit. It was all incredible! And

then a rush of air through my hair and past my ears drew my
attention. I had only a brief sensation of "lifting," wondering whether the wind was doing this to me; whether this
was an illusion like when I have walked out in a blizzard
and experienced a "white out" and thought I was walking up-
hill and was really going down.

And then, it all stopped as in meditation--the voices,
the questions. He motioned for me to follow and it seemed
the right thing to do. I walked or "floated" along behind
him as we made our way back to my cave.

When he finally spoke, it wasn't so much a voice as a
feeling of a message being received in my head. He spoke
for a long time and I could only listen in awe at the wonders
of the past and the future he described to me.

"You are one of the chosen ones," he said. "You are a
born teacher of the way." He told me of my future, of the
secrets of initiation, and of enlightenment.

"There are three sources of enlightenment," he said,
"love, knowledge, and power--and all of these are truth.
The love of truth brings knowledge and power. The knowledge
of truth brings the power of love. The power of truth brings
the knowledge of love. For truth is all in one."

Many more things were revealed to me that day and for the
first time in my life, I experienced perfect peace with myself
and my fellow humans. I was changed.

"Because Humankind and the Earth are spiritually con-
nected, what is done to the Earth will affect the lives of all
people in the future. All the turmoil that has arisen,
because Society has been unresponsive to the individual differences between races, and hatred between religions, results
in similar turmoil in the Earth.

"First, new lands will arise in the Pacific and Atlantic
oceans. Then, when there is intense volcanic activity on
Mt. Vesuvius and Mt. Celtna, an inundation of the southern
coast of California in America will occur.

"Water will appear across areas where no water was be-
fore--Greenland, Nevada, Northern Europe.

"Even now, parts of ancient Atlantis are being discovered once again near Bimini Island off the coast of Florida.

"The Mississippi will become much larger and become an
inland sea. The Great Lakes will empty into this sea as the
land tilts toward the South. New York will disappear as
earthquakes shake the upper portions of the eastern coast of
America. Land will appear off the southern tip of South
America, causing a strait of running water and eventually a
land bridge to the continent of Antarctica.

"You must be ready. You must prepare a community of
people with beliefs similar to yours. You must begin schools
and centers of learning to prepare leaders and teachers for
the New Age.

"Your people must be ready. They must prepare their
minds, souls, and bodies. They must prepare for the New Age--
a New Age of peace, harmony, and joy among all peoples. Those
who are not prepared will be unable to exist in the changed
world.

"You, Rhuddlwm, are to make your way to Georgia during the
next ten years. There you will begin your teaching.

"At first you will make many mistakes, and make many
enemies. But these enemies will eventually become friends.
You will teach those who will themselves become teachers.

"Even though it will look as if these people have no
teaching ability, they too will learn by doing.

"Rhuddlwm, you are a teacher of those who would teach.
You are a catalyst. You will cause many actions to take
place, affecting many people and leading them into a way that
many will be unprepared to handle. But fear not--others will
help you.

"Your greatest danger will be the tendency of many to
think of you as more than you are or less than you are.

"You are important--you are a leader and a reincarnated
Priest of ancient Atlantis. But it is not for anyone else

96

to know who else you are until the time is ripe.

"Certain people will contact you. Among them, a woman from California who will show you your feminine self, a woman from the midwest who will validate your search for a key, and a woman from Georgia who will aid you greatly and become a teacher in her own right. Prepare yourself--for they are "the Keys!"

"Because of your karmic imbalance women will be your lesson for the rest of your term on this plane.

"There will be many locations around the Earth where the people will find safety. Illinois, Indiana, Virginia, parts of Canada, parts of Africa, and these are but a few. But you will create a survival center in North Georgia, where all races and philosophies will be welcome.

"For remember, all is One. Every religion is based on the concept of the one true religion, and this concept shall be your starting point.

"Love, Knowledge, and Wisdom--Seek them out in everything you do and everywhere you go. You will find them, and use them in service of the Great Spirit."

As he finished speaking, I suddenly began to feel dizzy and nauseous, but the feeling seemed to last only a brief moment.

Suddenly the universe exploded in colors and shapes beyond description. I found myself plummeting down a long tunnel of colors and sounds, bright but cloudy, like a mist of flames, or rather what seemed to be flames, and an instant later the flames were within my own being. This was followed by a sense of exultation, ecstacy, and a complete enlightenment of my mind. The universe was a Living Being! I was part of this eternal life and through me all Humanity was immortal. I became conscious of the cosmic order and the striving for balance within all things. I saw that love was the foundation upon which the world was created, and that we as souls would all eventually achieve absolute happiness.

What was his name? The man with the dark hair and piercing eyes? The man with the shining brow and the flowing

97

white robe that shimmered in the sunlight? Our teacher says
that he is my spirit guide and that he will be with me
always. I call him Charlie. Sometimes when I am at my
wits end, I find him near. I talk to him and he either pushes
or prods me in the right direction. For Charlie is many
things to me. He is a companion when I'm alone, and he is
a confidante. He refuses to let anything really terrible
happen to me.

A spectre, you say? A hallucination? No, I think not.
Because Charlie comes only if I call him. Sometimes, I know
he's around watching me, but most of the time I'm on my own.

Although it has been several years since this sublime
experience, there have been others:

When I directed a particularly worthy seeker, or while
I conducted a particularly meaningful circle ritual.

There has always been a feeling of surprise and amaze-
ment over the awesome revelations which have been given to me,
and I experienced a sense of overwhelming gratitude and
wonder which will always be with me.

The knowledge gained through these experiences have
infused and affected every aspect of my life. They are as
real to me as the air we breathe or the food we eat. For
me, to doubt their validity is to doubt life itself.

Did I really see Charlie? Did I float six inches off the
ground? Did all these things really happen? I will always
believe that they did, because the experience changed me in
ways that are unexplainable. I know when things are going to
happen before they do. I see things in dreams which allow me
to know some aspects of the future. I can find things others
lose. I can read the thoughts and emotions of others. I have
predicted the flip of a coin twenty-three times in a row.
But, unfortunately, I'm not consistent. Although I have
experienced and continue to experience strange and wonderful
things, sometimes I can control them but at other times I
can't.

What is initiation? Is it what I experienced on that
mountain top or is it the ritual where I was "named" and
"adopted"? I believe it was a mixture of the two, for I
can't recall the exact moment when enlightenment came--
when truth poured into my mind. I do know that I went to
Wales a confused kid who used people and acted out of selfishness and vanity; I returned experiencing feelings of peace and
joy I had never known.

I thought back two weeks to my "naming."

* * * * *

Sarah was speaking:

"Initiation can be defined as the gradual entry of an
individual into the stream of life which is the source of
all divine manifestations. To be an initiate means to
consciously participate in the creative unfoldment of the
goals and visions of the planetary Guardian. This planet is
a living being, the body of an entity known as the planetary
spirit, Lugh. It is the custodian of a stream of cosmic
energy which we understand as life and is responsible for the
evolution of the consciousness of this world. Initiation is
not a reward, nor a ceremony, nor a fantasy. It is the conscious evocation of the fire of will. It moves with
inexorable purpose toward the consumption of its goal--
nothing less than the complete appropriation and infusion of
the physical, emotional, and mental vehicles of the personality.
True will is not a force. It is more like a presence of
irresistible power which transcends space and time. It simply
is, and when involved, stands and shatters whatever forms
are not in balance with what it is. In the words of an
initiate, 'Will is like a thunderbolt which conveys a sense
of dynamic power coupled with a rhythm of infinite peace and
patience.'"

Sarah continued:

"Should everyone become initiated into the Old Religion
and tread this path of enlightenment?" she asked herself and

99

then answered, "No! Enlightenment is not meant for everyone. 'Ignorance is bliss' someone said one, and to some extent it is true. For, when one becomes aware of all the greed, corruption, and evil which fills the world, one necessarily is opposed to it or succumbs to it. Only those who would fly to the moon or climb the highest mountain, only those who would do the impossible--the explorers of the unknown--the kind ones who see a little good in everyone--the patient ones who wait for the flower to open in the Spring, who take time to show a young child how to make a kite--only those who have the humanity within them already--only those are ready.

"All of the ancient masters were initiated--Jesus, Mohammed, Buddah, Confucius, and Moses to name a few. These superior humans saw the truth and tried to lead others to the same path. But, as soon as they died, their followers defied them, changed their teachings, and killed those who they could not convert--all in the name of peace and brotherhood.

"Do the churches teach peace and brotherhood and love today? Not many. For every church with an enlightened minister or priest there are a hundred who teach fear and damnation instead of 'love thy neighbor.' Some churches prey on the superstitions of their members and forbid them to associate with non-believers, even though by example, their Lord 'went even among the sinners' to heal the sick and feed the hungry.

"Are you ready for initiation? Are you ready for sacrifice? Are you ready to live your religion instead of just knowing what religion you are a member of? Are you ready to help those who would curse you and love those who would despise you? Are you ready to accept all religions as the same religion? Are you ready to assume the responsibilities for each and every one of your actions?

"Then know this: there is only one way to reach enlightenment--through initiation. But, in preparation one must accomplish three things. You must have been named,

100

accepting our pathway and taking a Welsh name as a symbol of this acceptance. You must go on your Quest, an ordeal of self denial and spiritual discipline which will carry over into your life as a hunger for knowledge, and finally, you must be adopted, which is a symbol of your inner transformation and our acceptance of you.

"To be named is to choose the pathway of Y Tylwyth Teg. This is the first step on a long and difficult journey. You will experience many sensations on your journey. You will feel the touch of love, drink the wine of Nature, hear the bell of keening, and see the light of understanding. You will learn of truth and beauty, and you will feel loneliness. You will discover that loneliness is really the fear of an unknown which is our inner self. Once you have passed through this barrier of loneliness, your sense of isolation will burst and you will feel a mystical identity with the universe.

"These experiences are but the symbols of the beginning of a process called initiation. By choosing a name which suits you and has special meaning for you, you are symbolically discarding all the outward trappings of ignorance and selfishness. You are then symbolically reborn as an enlightened one.

"When you depart on your Quest, you will be alone, with no food or other sustenance. You must seek out a place of running water and remain in one spot for several days drinking only water and meditating on your spiritual name. This fast is a spiritual purification which will prepare you for the vision of your spirit guide. This vision will make a strong imprint on your soul and bring meaning to your life.

"The Quest is also a means of integrating the right or intuitive side of your brain with the left, or analytical side. This condition is temporary at first but with training and practice, 'dual integration' will be a permanent condition of your being.

"The Quest enables you to communicate directly with your higher Self, and to know your true destiny. Prepare yourself well, seeker, for with the Quest, you enter upon a new aspect of your life.

"Seekers, with the 'rite of adoption' you complete that which is required for the first level of Gwidion, or 'wise one,' also known by the ancients as 'Witch' or 'Magus.'

"'Adoption' is our acceptance of the seeker as one of the Family and one of the tribe. By adopting the seeker, we give that seeker the protection of the family and orally transmit the thirteen treasures--the secret wisdom of the Cymmry.

"Within the adoption ritual is the symbolism of the thirteen treasures, the hidden people, the initiation. This is the third rite, and the ending of the beginning.

"The mystery of initiation can only take place if the secret force of its symbols is hidden from the profane eyes of the world. The moment we try to analyze the initiation experience, the concepts seem to become as water falling upon the desert sand. For although nothing is secret in the initiation process, one must experience it to understand it. By trying to explain what is beyond mere words, we profane what is essentially a sacred experience.

"Initiation is a death and a resurrection--the death of rigidity of our ordinary personality, and your preconditioning and the resurrection of your higher self. One must learn self-trust and self-expression, that is not constrained by ideals. For true freedom will lead to right action and perfection by providing the greatest occasion for experience and choice.

"Only in this way may you discover the will of the Spirit of Humankind. In the religion of Y Tylwyth Teg, Nature is the creative spirit in this world. Therefore, there is no basic conflict between Nature and the spirit. In other religions, Nature is something to subdue. In the Old Religion,

102

worship of the Great Mother acknowledges the profound wisdom
of Nature, which controls the process of cosmic evolution.
Just as the Great Mother represents the external experience
of Nature, there is within one's own inner consciousness a
deep wisdom which is the inner experience of Nature. This
inner experience is the first step on the pathway to enlightenment."

* * * * *

The priestess began speaking:

"You who are about to be named, this is a very important
step in your life. If you are not completely sure now,
speak out--for after this point there is no turning back.

"William, this is a sacred and spiritual occasion.
This is the point where you commit yourself to a way of
life filled with numerous trials but also with rewards that
are not imaginable to the normal human being. This ritual
demands your trust and confidence.

"William, welcome, for you are recognized as a Seeker
after Truth, and as a Seeker you have come before us to be
named. In your naming is intertwined the symbolism of our
Clan.

"As a Seeker, you have shown your worthiness by actions,
deeds, and words. The name you have chosen will be yours
until you pass from this plane of existence into the next,
and will mean, 'one who seeks.' .Whenever you think of your
clan name you will also think, 'I seek.'

"William, what is it you seek?"

"Enlightenment."

"Throughout your naming, you will encounter symbolism
which will help you to progress along the path of enlightenment.
You are blindfolded, therefore you cannot see to seek. You
are naked, as the day you were born. You are afraid, for
behind the darkness is the unknown. You are bound, as all are
bound by inhibitions before they set out on the path. For the
meaning of the naming is this: You are blind and confused,

103

losing our way. Through suffering and labor, you regain the path and pass the test, opening the inner mind to the awareness of a new plane of existence.

"You will experience many sensations on your journey. You will taste the wine of Nature, inhale the sacred Incense, hear the bell of Keening, feel the touch of Love, and see the Light of Understanding."

I felt the point of a knife at my chest.

"William, what are the pass words to admit you to the Circle of Enlightenment?"

As I said them, the point of the blade withdrew from me.

"Welcome, Seeker."

I was then brought into the Circle. I was introduced to the four quarters of the Circle and then following a complex ritual of awakening, the priestess said, "William, what name have you chosen?"

"Rhuddlwm Gawr."

"Ancient ones, this one has named himself Rhuddlwm Gawr, which from this moment on shall mean 'one who seeks.' Protect him from all harm."

The bell was rung, the blindfold was removed, and we drank wine as the priestess chanted:

"Ancient ones, as we drink of this fruit of the vine, so may we be changed even as this fruit was changed."

At the conclusion of the ritual, the covenant was sealed with the "Sacred Rite."

Blessed Mother

105

CHAPTER EIGHT

THE FESTIVALS

"It is worth noting that the original purpose of
ritual was to order the life of the community in
harmony with the forces of nature (TAO), on which
subsistence and well-being depended." --Mai-Mai Sze

It was the morning before Gwyl Canol Gaef or Yule.
I had lived in the village for six months now. It was to be
my first festival. I was not allowed to attend Gawyl Gaef
(November Eve), or Samhain, and I was extremely nervous.

The other novice seekers and I were gathered in the
great hall. In beautiful ceremonial robes, her arms expanding in warm gestures, the Elder spoke:

"Of old, our festivals have been a time of celebration
of the cycles of Nature and placing our minds in communion
with the Great Spirit. We return power and energy to the
Deities and ourselves through the seasonal festivals, just
as we call upon the Deities to raise power during the Full
Moon rituals.

"Always remember, as we take energy from Nature, we
must also return energy to Nature. Although many religions
have sacred festivals, not all know of their origins. When
the first pure humans were yet both male and female, or 'two
in one,' they had mental power and abilities far beyond
those of people today. Humans could move objects with their
minds, and they freely interchanged thoughts among themselves.
The past, present, and future were as one. The source of
this power was with the Great Spirit; and the God and Goddess,
manifested through the forces of Nature; and the Sun, the
Moon, the Planets and stars.

"As humankind gradually separated into two sexes, human
mental powers became lost and hidden. People became aware

106

"The Worship of the Moon in all its Aspects"

that their powers were lessening, and tried to regain these abilities through contact with the Great Spirit through the God and Goddess, the Lord and lady.

"They found that they could make contact through 'power nodes' existing at certain locations on the earth's surface. The nodes are most active at the times of the Full Moon, New Moon, Solstice, and Equinox. Today, these power nodes are still being activated by ancient tradition, through our rituals and festivals.

"These power nodes release a psychic impulse called the Odic Force. This force can be controlled by visualization of symbols, by singing, by chanting, and by dancing.

"We will first explore the seasonal festivals or Sabbats. During the festivals, the seeker returns energy to Nature by experiencing a condition of ecstasy closely related to states of meditation and hypnosis. The idea at this time is to send mental energy back to the God/dess. This is a time of joy and a time of happiness. We give thanks to Nature for its sustenance and we perform dances and sing for our crops to grow tall. We make love to one another in imitation of the Great Mother, Queen of Fertility, and Pan, King of the Wood. The energy released will aid them in their many tasks."

As we arrived at the Grove, the High Priest and High Priestess were constructing the circle with the help of the Candlebearer and the Maiden. A circle was measured twenty feet in diameter, using a string with one end looped around a wooden peg driven into the ground, and the other end looped around a wand. Next, a narrow trench was dug approximately six inches deep around the perimeter of the circle.

One of the Elders was speaking:

"The number twelve signifies all and is applied to religious truth. Thirty degrees signify the fullness of truth and goodness found in a person in his other natural state. Each degree is marked with the stone on the inside of

108

circle and a wooden peg on the outside of the trench opposite
the stone. The trench surrounding the circle is filled with
water and represents the sea. The trench is that portion
of our grove-temple which represents natural worship in its'
external form."

Lanterns using perfumed and blessed candles were then
placed on the ground at the four quarters of the circle.
At the center of the circle was the altar, and upon the altar
was placed the Cauldron of Inspiration. Three candles were
positioned around the cauldron--North, East, and West.

The altar was constructed of a flat stone and two
supporting stones which were placed East and West at the
center of the circle. The High Priest poured the sacred
spring water into the Cauldron which had been blessed previously. The High Priest then cast the sacred herbs into
the water and a ripple of light spread over them before they
disappeared.

The festival was beginning as the High Priest sheathed
a sword with the words, "Y gwir yn erbyn y byd," (Truth
against the world). As the sword was laid upon the altar,
the Archoffeiriades faced the East in the direction of the
rising sun and chanted the words, "Iao...Iao...Iao. Join
us as one, we who are male and female."

The High Priestess played the telyn harp while the
Gwillion danced clockwise around the outside of the trench.
At the end of the song, twelve Gwillion positioned themselves
in front of the twelve pegs, and called the guardians. The
High Priestess chanted the words three times as the High Priest
lit each lantern. The chanting seemed to swell into an ex-
plosion of light. Each time the words were spoken, a seeker
placed a flower by a lantern.

"Y dwyrain--Oh ancient watcher of the East, protect us,
we who evoke you. Guard this circle and let no evil pass.

"Y dehev--Oh ancient watcher of the South, protect us,
we who evoke you. Guard this circle and let no evil pass.

109

"Y gorllewin--Oh ancient watcher of the West, protect us, we who evoke you. Guard this circle and let no evil pass."

"Y gogledd--Oh ancient watcher of the North, protect us, we who evoke you. Guard this circle and let no evil pass."

The High Priestess, lighting the balefire to the North of the altar, held an expression of mystical union with the Goddess. All faced toward it as she said:

"Io Evo He!"

All: "Io Evo He!"

High Preistess: "Io Evo He!"

All: "Io Evo He!"

High Priestess: "Io Evo He!"

All: "Io Evo He! Blessed Be!"

At the altar, the incense was ignited.

High Priestess: "Oh, Great Cerridwen, Queen of Light, spread your fragrance through all the night!"

All: "Blessed Be!"

The three candles on the altar were lit.

High Priest: "Oh Goddess of love and life, bring down your power upon this your altar and bless it for our use. It is an altar dedicated to you, our lady. Io Evo He! Blessed Be! Io Evo He! Blessed Be!"

All: "Blessed Be!"

The twelve Gwillion entered the circle as the High Priestess invoked the Blessing of the Goddess. Holding the wand in her right hand, arms crossed on her breast, she spoke:

"I, Rhiannon, Goddess of all life, call down the universal blessings upon this temple. May all who partake of these rites be welcomed into the clan of the Fairy Folk. Peace, Health, and Love in abundance are yours and wisdom shall fill your soul."

At this point the hair was standing up on the back of my head and I was tingling all over!

The High Priest proclaimed:

"Listen to the words of the Great Mother, who was of old called among men, Artemis, Astarte, Aphrodite, Arionhod,

110

Branwen, Cerridwen, Diane, Melusin, and by many other names."

The High Priestess replied:

"At my altars the youth of Lacedamon in Sparta made sacrifice, and I instructed them thus: Whenever ye have need of anything, once in the month, but better it be when the Moon is full, assemble in some secret place, ye who are fain to learn all sorcery, yet have not won its deepest secrets. To thee will I teach all things that are yet unknown.

"Ye shall be free from slavery, and as a sign of your freedom, ye shall be naked in your rites, and ye shall dance, sing, make music and love, all in my praise. For mine is the ecstasy of the spirit, and mine is also the joy on earth, for my law is love unto all beings.

"Keep pure your highest ideals, strive ever toward them, let naught stop you or turn you aside. For mine is the door which opens upon the secret of youth, and mine is the cup of the wine of life, and the Cauldron of Cerridwen which is the Holy Grail of Immortality.

"I am the gracious Goddess who gives the gift of joy unto the heart of man. Upon earth I give the knowlege of the spirit eternal, and beyond death, give peace and freedom and reunion with those who have gone before. Nor do I demand sacrifice, for behold, I am the Mother of all living things and my love is poured out upon the earth!"

Ancient flasks and cups were used to pour water into the trench, and then the High Priest faced East from the altar and raised his athame while all the rest of us also faced East and raised our athames.

It was a time of silence and waiting. In those moments, the clear night expanded into irridescent shades of dark purple-blue as in a harvest of grapes. Gold-bronze skin tones rolled above the fire in wonderful complement.

The High Priest chanted:

"Lugh, Lugh, Lugh, Oh Lord of Light, come and dance with us. Descend upon us and bless us. Enter here into your

111

dwelling." He touched the altar with his athame. "Bring joy into us as we join together in thy name."

We all now faced the altar, athames sheathed and hands clasped in front. The High Priestess faced the altar from the South and raised the water and wine as the circle melted and released its shape.

We all sang:

"Here we bring new water, here we bring old wine. For to worhip Cerridwen as the Moon doth shine. Sing reign of a fair maiden, with gold upon her toe, open ye the Moon Gate and let the West Wind blow. Sing reign of a fair maiden, with gold upon her chin, open yet the North Gate and let Cerridwen in. Sing levez dew, levez dew, ye water and ye wine. Hail to fair Cerridwen whose ancient Moon doth shine."

The High Priestess now raised the salt and corn as we sang:

"Here the dish of corn we bring,
Here the salt of Earth.
Blessed meal of labouring,
Blessed salt of worth.
Fairie Queen steal through the night,
Silver wings aglow with dew.
Dance ye wee folk in delight,
Drwy Y nos, canu,
Drwy Y nos, canu."

She raised the plate of cakes as we then sang:

"Here the Sabbat cakes of grain,
Baked upon the hearth,
Blessed be the feast of Cain,
Dance in joy and mirth."

She raised the honey as the voices rose:

"Here we bring the honey sweet,
Gathered from the sacred grove.
Dawnsio, dawnsio, little bees!
Keep to your hives and do not roam."

The spiral dance began, and our bodies were shining
with perspiration before it was over. It was now time to
celebrate the feast. Cakes and wine were served within
the temple. The people chanted in unison:

"With this blessed wine we infuse our bodies with the
life blood which flows through all things. Let this wine be
the manifest essence of all the blessed elements. Bless
these your children, O Great Lugh and Cerridwen, who have
gathered here to manifest your power. Let us know the delight
and fulfillment that is your gift to those who practice your
rites. So Mote It Be!"

As the High Priestess passed the cakes, we again chanted
in unison:

"With these cakes we consume the body and the life force
of the Lord and Lady, which are our sustenance. Give us love
and joy, which shall be ours forever."

The feast now commenced in earnest with dancing, singing,
food in abundance, and love-making. The Gwillion jumped over
the Balefire symbolizing the purification of their souls by
fire.

At the end of the festival, the four guardians were
thanked and released. The sword was unsheathed with the words,
"Y gwin yn erbyn y byd," and the circle was closed.

We returned to our cottages and rooms, the darkness
flowing into the gentleness of dawn, the silence of the night
and the trees enclosing us. A full circle was completed;
vision, study, endurance, meditation, celebration. The moon
was gone now, the day approached, and time was measured in
shafts of pale light on the rocks.

The next day we learned the Seasonal Variations to the
festivals. Our Guide began:

"The festival of the Eve of November which is All Hallows
Eve--Halloween--is the beginning of the Dewenieth Cymmry year.
Ruled by the Lord, this is the final harvest and also the
festival of the spirits. It is the death of summer and a time

113

of communing with loved ones who have passed away.

"The colours are orange and black. The symbols are all autumn fruits and plants. The pumpkin is the symbol of the last fruit of the Lady.

"This is the celebration of the strengthening of Lleu the Long Handed, God of the Rising Sun. Wagon wheels are wrapped with straw dipped in tar, set alight, and sent blazing down a hillside for good luck in the coming year.

"Gwyl Canol Gaeor, The Yule Festival, is the festival of the Sun God and is the shortest day of the year. It is the time for the rebirth of the Sun.

"The nature symbols are holly, mistletoe, pine boughs, ivy, and evergreen plants. The balefire, made up of the nine sacred woods, is lit. The colours are red, green, and white. Red for the heat of Lugh, the God of the Sun; green for the evergreen leaves to remind us that spring will return; and white for the unending truth of the Great Spirit which aids our search for the pathway.

"The wheel of life has turned full circle. This is the resurrection of our Lord, Pam.

"Gwyl Fair, The Festival of Branwen, is the celebration of the Goddess's recovery from giving birth to the young Sun God. This is the festival of the waxing light. The first flowers of the year are placed on the altar as a dedication to the God/dess.

"The nine sacred woods are laid for the balefire. The colours are red, yellow, and white. Red for the heart, yellow for the warmth of the Sun, and white for eternal light. Initiations are traditionally given at this time.

"Gwyl Granwyn, the Rites of Spring, is the celebration of the awakening of Mother Nature and all her children. Nature is again fertile and is reflected in humanity, crops, and animals. Spring flowers are the sacrifice. The balefire is lighted.

"The colors are green, white, and blue. The green is of nature, the white of the eternal light, and the blue of

114

the sky. The blessing of the seeds is performed at this time.

"Gwyl Canol Hef, Midsummer Festival, is the middle of summer--the halfway point in the celestial year. The colours are green, red, and blue. Our symbols are first harvest fruits, lemons, oranges, roses, etc. The oak is the sacred tree. The balefire is lighted. This is the celebration of the battle between the Sons of Light and the Sons of Darkness.

"Noswyl Awst, August Eve, is the first grain harvest festival and is a sacrificial feast. Various dances are performed. The first harvest from the grain is baked into bread and cakes which are sweetened with honey and eaten with sacred wine at a love feast. The Lady is preparing to rest. The colours are yellow, red, and white.

"Gwyl Hydref, Fall Festival, is the second harvest festival and celebrates our Lord's return from Gwlad Yr Hav, the Summerland. The colours are orange, red, and brown. Our Lady is resting. The symbols are fruits of the second harvest.

* * * * *

Finally, the time came for us to celebrate our first Full Moon Ritual. We stood outside the circle as the High Priestess prepared the altar. It was cold and we were all shivering. When all was ready, we began to enter the circle.

"Halt, seeker! Why attempt you to enter the Temple of the Cymmry?" challenged the High Priestess.

"I seek enlightenment."

"All who seek Enlightenment also know two words."

"Knowlege and Power," I said firmly.

"Seeker, enter in perfect love and perfect trust and may the Blessings of Branwen be upon thee."

She touched my forehead with oil, making the sign of the Celtic Cross, then kissed me on the cheek.

When we had positioned ourselves alternately, male-female, around the inside of the circle, the High Priest began the "Calling Down of the Moon" upon the High Priestess.

115

"I invoke thee and call upon thee, O Mighty Mother of us all, bringer of fruitfulness, by seed and by root, by stem and by bud.

"I invoke thee by Life and by love and call upon thee to descend into the body of this thy Priestess. Speak with her tongue, touch with her hands, see with her eyes, and kiss with her lips, that thy children may be fulfilled."

The High Priestess then assumed the Goddess position, as the High Priest drew down the Moon by the force of his concentration and prayer.

He then touched her on the breast and womb, turning to face us, saying:

"Hear the words of the Great Mother, who was of old called among men Artemis, Astarte, Dione, Melusine, Aphrodite, Cerridwen, Diane, Arionhod, Branwen, and by many other names."

The High Priestess then replied:

"At my altar, the youths of Lacedemon in Sparta made due sacrifice. Whenever ye have need of anything, once in the month, and best it be when the Moon is full, then shall ye assemble in some secret place and adore the spirit of me, who am Queen of all the Witcheries. There shall ye assemble, who are feign to learn all sorceries, who have not as yet won my deepest secrets.

"These will I teach that which is yet unknown. And ye shall be free from all slavery and as a sign that ye be free, ye shall be naked in your rites and shall sing, feast, make music and love, all in mine presence. For mine is the ecstasy of the spirit and mine is also joy on earth, for my law is love for all beings. Keep pure your highest ideals, strive ever toward them. Let none stop you or turn you aside. For mine is the secret that opens upon the door of youth and mine is the cup of the wine of life and the Cauldron of

116

Cerridwen, which is the Holy Grail of Immortality. I am
the Gracious Goddess who gives the gift of love into the
heart of man upon earth. I give the knowledge of the spirit
eternal as beyond death I give peace and freedom and reunion
with those who have gone before. Nor do I demand aught in
sacrifice, for behold, I am the Mother of all living things,
and mine love is poured out upon the earth."

The High Priest then rang the ritual bell three times,
saying:

"Comes now the ritual of the Moon."

The High Priest walked to the Maiden at the East Watchtower, saying:

"The young virgin. She comes to her awakening, a time
of rebirth, hands out-stretched towards the stars."

The 1st Maiden replied:

"Behold me
  For I am the Young Virgin
  Giving birth to myself
  Born unto myself
  One-In-Myself.
  For I come as the Spring comes
  Tremulous with her new born flowers,
  Hungry and still innocent
  As the first birdlings.
  I am as the faery queen's daughter,
  Born into etheric joyfulness
  Coming at last into my own
  For I am completed in Love's arms."

The High Priest chanted:

"And Spring moves gaily into Summer and Summer is born
in her time of awakening."

The High Priest walked to the maiden in the South.

"The Lover--She comes to her awakening, a time of rebirth,
hands cupping breasts."

117

The 2nd Maiden replied:

"Behold me, I am the lover
 The union of light and dark.
 I am the interaction between opposites.
 The manifestation of time and creation.
 The long flames of silken fire envelope
 Me in rapturous ecstasy.
 I am in the summer of my life.
 Sweet as the sun ripened peaches upon the tree.
 I am the enchantress.
 I speak the body language,
 Words of splendored Love.
 To enter my door is to enter the temple,
 On the wings of the butterfly.
 Fly towards me--
 If in your heart only.
 For I am completed in Love's arms."

"And Summer moves lightly into Fall and Fall is born in her time of awakening." The High Priest then moved to the Maiden at the West Watchtower and said:

"The Mother--She comes to her awakening, a time of re-birth, hands across a full belly."

The 3rd Maiden replied:

"Behold me
 I am the Mother
 With her bountiful harvest.
 My breasts ache in their fullness.
 I reach for the child's mouth,
 Gladly and with joyful sacrifice.
 I am serene and I nurture mine own,
 And are not all mine own!
 I am in the fall of my life
 And my boundless heart waits
 Patiently for all who call
 My name.
 For I am completed in Love's arms."

118

"And Fall moves tenderly into Winter and Winter is
born in her time of awakening," said the High Priest as he
moved to the Maiden at the North Watchtower.

"The Wise Woman--She comes to her awakening, a time of
rebirth, hands across her loins."

The 4th Maiden replied:

"Behold me, I am the Wise Woman.
  I who have given birth to myself,
  I who have been the silken fire,
  I who have tended the fruits of my labour
  Am now revered, and yes, oft times feared.
  For my years of gathered wisdom lay
  Heavy as snow on my bowed shoulders.
  I have no need of youth's illusion,
  I am in the winter of my life,
  And all is white stillness around me.
  Yet, I too move with inner life,
  For I am completed in Love's arms."

"And Winter moves slowly into Spring and the cycle continues. We ebb and flow, contract and expand. And Space--
Time--Creation dance to the music with arms of love."

"She dreams."

The High Priest rang the bell three times.

"Comes now the feast."

He held up the wine to the East, saying:

"I bring ye wine from above
From the vats of the storied Sun,
For every one of ye love
And life for every one.
Ye shall dance on hill and level.
Ye shall sing in hollow and height.
In the festival mystical revel,
The rapturous Bacchanal rite!"

The High Priestess then took the cup and knelt in front
of the High Priest, who placed his athame into the cup,
saying:

119

"As the athame is to the male, so the cup is to the female. As shown, so below. As the beginning, so the end. As the Sun, so the Earth.

"Bless this wine, O Mother of all, and consecrate its purpose to the life's blood of your children."

The High Priestess drank from the cup and passed it to the High Priest, who after drinking, passed it around the circle. After all had drank, the High Priestess drained the cup except for a few drops which she let fall on the earth.

The High Priest presented the cakes on the plate to the High Priestess who blessed them with her athame.

The High Priest lifted the cakes, and said:

"O mighty Branwen, Bless this food to the nourishment of our bodies, bestowing all that is good upon us."

The High Priestess took the cakes and ate while the High Priest passed the remaining cakes around the circle-- again, crumbs were returned to the earth.

With warm and nourished bodies we performed a Healing ritual, after which we danced, feasted, and made love in the darkness.

The ritual had ended.

CHAPTER 9
The Horned One

CHAPTER NINE

THE NINE LEVELS OF THE MYSTIC PATH

"Whatever is attained, always ask--Is there anything
more?" --Rhuddlwm Gawr

Learning and reading continued on into the winter,
and the coals glowed brightly when we retired each night.
New dimensions opened up from the study of ancient lessons.
I disciplined myself in the new knowledge.

"Within Y Tylwyth Teg, there are nine steps to ultimate
enlightenment. Each of these nine levels is symbolic of
the attainment of sufficient love, knowledge, and power to
advance to the next," Sarah said musically.

"The clan of Y Tylwyth Teg is ruled by Y Beirdd Cyfrin,
or the 'mystic bards' who represent the groves, or covens,
in open council. All seekers of levels seven, eight, and
nine are members of Y Cylch Cyfrin, or the mystic circle,
and govern all disputes between clans within the tribe, or
cantreff, of Dynion Mwyn (Gentle Folk)." She paused for a
moment.

"The Brenin, or chief of the tribe of Dewiniaeth Cymmry,
is the secret leader who has advanced to level nine. In
individual groves, or celli, a council of three elders of
level three or above govern by suggestion, but rarely by
decree. The Archoffieriades and Archoffieriade (High Priestess
and Priest), elected by the membership from among those of
level two, are the leaders of the grove. The Archoffieriade
appoints a kanuylyt, or candlebearer, and the Archoffieriades
appoints a lavoruyn, or handmaiden, from those members of
level one."

We were trying to take notes as she rapidly continued.

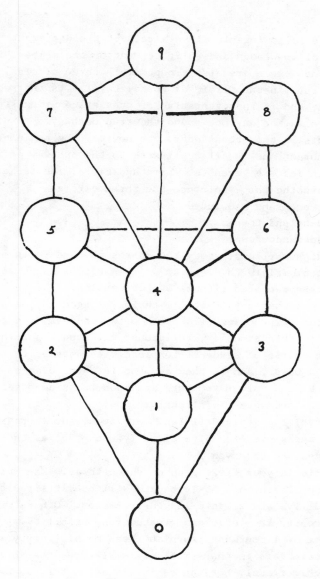

The Nine Steps

123

"The following nine levels reflect the different
degrees of knowledge and enlightenment of the membership.
These nine levels are also grouped into three circles.

"First, in the Circle of Poets, Level 0 is the seeker
(Awenydd) and is representative of that stage of existence
where the seeker has not found the true pathway.

"This is the probationer, the novice, the beginner,
'the ignorant one.' All applicants to the pathway of
Y Tylwyth Teg are given this name and title. The seeker
must learn the three columns--the three circles.

Strength and Knowledge

Beauty and Love

Wisdom and Power

"The seeker must study the philosophy and religious
precepts of Y Tylwyth Teg, as well as become adept at performing the required rituals and ceremonies. The seeker
must study: history, Celtic mythology, paganism, meditation,
nature magick, the sexual aspects of Witchcraft, seasonal
festivals, reincarnation, religious philosophy, and initiation.
When the course of study i: completed, the seeker is named,
goes on a Quest, and is then adopted into the clan of
Y Tylwyth Teg. All of you here are soon to be adopted."

We grinned ever so slightly.

"Level 1 is the 'Gwillion,' or witch, and is representative of the seeker's choice of 'Y Tylwyth Teg' as the pathway,
symbolized by the raven.

"This is your first step on the pathway. Many of you
will never leave this position and will be satisfied to stay
here and live and worship in your religion. Others will go
on to greater knowledge and greater responsibility.

"The Gwillion must learn the meaning of liberty, equality,
and unity. This is the symbol of initiation--the spiritual
and psychic ritual, but the real initiation for the Gwillion
may not occur for many years. Sometimes a Gwillion may
already be initiated before attempting the pathway.

124

Initiation happens in the mind and heart of the seeker and can never be bestowed. It must come from within. Although one may symbolically be initiated by the words and rituals of humanity, real initiation is only received at the hands of the Lord and Lady."

She looked intently at each of us.

"This is the position of preparation--the material step in dealing with material things, for all spiritual life must be raised upon a material foundation. Seven is the number of the first level, Gwillion, symbolic of mastery over the seven psychic centers of the human body. A Gwillion enters upon a path where knowledge of the reason that certain things are done certain ways is absent. Their duty is to follow the directions of others whose knowledge is greater than theirs. Through action and reaction, strength is built as well as the gift of Liberty, the knowledge of equality, and the desire for unity. Here one prepares to experience the God/dess."

She held up two fingers.

"Level 2 is the Priest/Priestess (Offieriade/Offieriades) who is ordained into the Priesthood or Offieriadaeth of Y Tylwyth Teg. The symbol is the occultist.

"The day will come when you must apply your knowledge. The key to this level is emotion and conquest of the spirit. This places the energy of the universe in your hands. This great power, which is necesary in leading a grove, can only be entrusted to those individuals who can prove their ability to use it constructively and selflessly. The High Priest or Priestess must master emotional outbreaks of all kinds, keep poised under trying conditions, show kindness in the face of unkindness, and demonstrate simplicity of life. The lower nature must be controlled, for the control and understanding of the creative forces is essential to the performance of the duties of this level.

125

"As one of the second level, you will prepare yourself
to become a teacher. To reach this point, you must obtain
the basic esoteric knowledge of the following subjects:
divination and the tarot, scrying, Celtic runes, clairvoyance,
sex magick, ceremonial magick, talismanic magick, hypnosis,
herb craft, massage, psychic healing, contemporary religions,
ancient philosophies, symbols and initiation. At this point,
you will experience the presence of the Lord and Lady."

She gave the sign of the broad arrow.

"Level 3 is the 'dysgawdr dos,' or teacher, and it is
at this point where the seeker gains authority to begin or
charter a new grove and to teach the precepts of the fairy
folk. The symbol is the warrior. This is a new birth.

"This is the point at which you learn the twelve virtues: tolerance, charity, humility, devotion, patience,
kindness, forbearance, sincerity, courage, precision,
efficiency, and discernment.

"This is the teacher of the young tree who stands on
the lower steps of spiritual unfolding. This is the pathway
through the outer circle of esoteric learning, but is now
also learning to teach others of the pathway. To reach this
point, you must master ancient folklore and keys to knowledge, Druidic philosophy, and the thirteen treasures of the
Welsh.

"This level is symbolic of the quest, where a hundred
difficulties will assail you and you will undergo a hundred
trials. It will take several years to reach this level,
making great efforts to change the state of your mind. You
must ask your cupbearer for a drink of wine and when you
have consumed it, nothing will matter except the quest.
Then you will no longer fear the dragons which guard the door
and which seek to devour you. When the door is opened and
you enter, dogma and belief, or lack of them, cease to exist.
This is the quest for the Cauldron of Inspiration."

126

She paused and asked for questions. Unbelievably,
there were none!

"The Mystic Bards, Y Beirdd Cyfrin, is the second
circle. Within the second circle, Level 4 is 'y mynechdid
cana,' or guide, and has the responsibility of mastering
one esoteric science. This guide becomes one of the mystic
bards and is allowed to represent the grove in open council.
The symbol is the lion and represents dedication.

"To reach this point, you must learn the meaning of:
study and application, bravery, devotedness, patriotism, pro-
tecting the oppressed, and devoting oneself to the honor and
interest of the tribe. The key here is Love. You must be
consumed by a flaming fire, for with love, good and evil
cease to exist. There is only truth. You must dedicate
yourself completely to your path or you will never be free
of the sadness which weighs you down.

"When love appears, reason disappears. Love has nothing
to do with reason. If you possess inner sight, you would
perceive the atoms and molecules of the visible world. But,
if you perceive the world with ordinary eyes, you will never
understand the necessity of love. Only one who has been
tested and is free from illusion can feel this. You must
master one esoteric science in order to reach this step.
This seeker must study clairovoyance and healing.

"To reach this pont, it is necessary to experience
the love of the God/dess."

She held up her hand, all fingers extended.

"Level 5 is 'y cawr clerwr,' or chief guide, and has
mastery over several esoteric sciences. One from this level
may be elected to office in the open council. The symbol
is the persian and represents a flight into darkness.

"This seeker must master understanding and learn the
meaning of: toleration and liberality against fanacticism
and persecution, education and enlightenment against error
and ignorance. One must devote one's hand, heart, and mind,

127

as well as be earnest, true, reliable, and sincere--True unto humanity, sincere in all things, and earnest in duty. Meditation on the 'Secret Word' is necessary.

"No pathway is equal to this plateau and the distance to be traveled in crossing it is beyond comprehension. Understanding is enduring, but knowledge is temporary. The soul is in a state of progress or decline, and the spiritual way reveals itself only in the degree to which the traveler has overcome the faults and weaknesses inherent in the way. You will approach nearer to your goal according to effort. If a mosquito were to fly with all it's might, could it equal the speed of the wind? When this road is illuminated by the sun, each receives light according to merit and finds a place assigned in the understanding of truth.

"The seeker receives oral teachings and learns of the Great Temples of our people, receives survival training, and specializes in ancient art and literature.

"Here you begin to understand the bi-polar religious philosophy of the threefold God and God/dess.

"Level 6 is the 'hebryngyat file ollamh,' or junior elder, who may attain to the supreme seat in open council by election.

"The keys of this level are independence and detachment. The seeker reflects and meditates on the symbols and learns secret oral knowledge. The motto is 'Seek and ye shall find.' This seeker obtains knowledge and truth and teaches knowledge and truth. The seeker learns fidelity to obligation, constancy, and perseverance. The seeker must vow to crusade against ignorance, intolerance, and error, but must do this quietly and secretly. At this level there is neither the desire to possess nor the wish to discover. In this state of the soul, a cold wind blows, so violent that in a moment it devastates an immense space. The seven oceans are no more than a pool, the seven planets are a mere spark, the seven heavens a corpse. There is balance between heart and head.

128

"At this level, nothing old or new has value, you can act or not. 'Human knowledge is but an imperfect reflection of the Infinite.'

"The seeker must master astrology, astronomy, physics, geology, geography, sociology, and a musical instrument. Here we discover the true aspect of the Lord and Lady.

"The Mystic Circle, Y Cylch Cyfrin, is the third circle. Level 7 is the 'tywysog/tywysoges aikas,' or chief elder, and becomes one of the mystic circle. At this point you are given the secret manuscripts of the family.

"This level teaches that man is immortal. The seeker must learn respect for labor, to improve the moral nature of the seeker, to acquire modesty and humbleness in accomplishment. The slogan here is 'Work through Unity.' Think with the heart, love with the hand.

"At this level, everything is broken into pieces and then unified. All who raise their heads here, raise them from the same position. Although you seem to see many beings, in reality there is only one. All make one which is complete in its unity. There is a full flowering of the higher centers.

"Again, that which is seen as a unity is not different from that which appears as a number. For the Great Spirit is beyond unity and numbering. Cease to think of eternity as before and after and since these two eternities have vanished, cease to speak of them. When all that is visible is reduced to nothing, what is there left to contemplate?

"Here you discover the unity of the Lord and Lady, the God and Goddess.

"Level 8 is 'y credadun anruth,' or believer of the noble stream. This one may be elected to lead the clan of Y Tylwyth Teg.

"This step leads to astonishment and bewilderment. Here you are prey to sadness and dejection. There are signs which cut like swords, and each breath is a bitter sigh. You experience sorrow and a burning eagerness. It is at once day

129

and night. There is fire, yet the seeker is depressed and
despondent. But, one who has achieved unity forgets, and
all forget themselves. If the seeker is asked, 'Are you
or are you not? Have you or have you not the feeling of
existence? Are you in the middle or on the border? Are
you mortal or immortal?,' the seeker will reply with certainty, 'I know nothing, I understand nothing, I am unaware of
myself. I am in love, but with whom I do not know. My
heart is, at the same time, both full and empty of love,'
There is attainment of soul wisdom.

"Here you will learn: all the mysteries, instructions
and symbols of the universal language. The motto here is,
'The Gods freely disclose their intentions to the wise, but
to the fool their teaching is unintelligible.' The seeker
must learn to reclaim the lessons in visible symbols, or in
those parables and dark sayings of old. The seeker learns
that we do not undervalue the importance of any truth. We
utter no word that can be deemed irreverent by any faith.

"The triads of the attributes of the ineffable one are
wisdom--strength--harmony. The seeker must understand: the
need for truth and loyalty, and that the universal consciousness rules the movement of the universe.

"Level 9 is the 'brenin,' or chief, of the tribe. This
is 'Y arweinydd cyfrin,' or secret leader--the Enlightened
One. To reach this level one must control the three essentials of 'gwron-plennyd-arawm.'

"The meaning of the Celtic Cross is discovered. The
seeker experiences humility, patience, and self-denial. This
is the trial.

"This step is impossible to describe. The essence of
this step is forgetfulness, blindness, deafness, and dis-
traction. Ten thousand shadows surrounding the seeker disappear in a triple ray from the Celestial Sun. When the
waves of the ocean begin to break, the pattern on its surface

130

loses form, and becomes the pattern of the world now and
to come. Whoever declares that they do not exist know
truth. The tiny drop that becomes part of the great ocean
stays there forever and in peace. In this calm sea, a human,
at first, experiences only humiliation and dissolution, but
emerging from this state, understands it as creation.

"Support yourself on that which resists, and separate
the artificial from the true. The seeker who travels this
pathway will discover absolute knowledge, love, and power."

Our minds were beginning to overflow with knowledge
which both warmed us and left us shivering with apprehension,
humility, and sensitivity.

Again, we listened silently.

"If you survive the nine levels, the great mysteries
will be revealed in advanced rituals:

"The Rite of Purification by living the life of the
seeker, this is love.

"The Rite of Illumination by developing clairvoyance
and clairaudience, this is knowledge.

"The Rite of Mastership which is the mystical marriage
between personality and spirit, this is power.

"Love--knowledge--power, the three essentials."

CHAPTER 10
Mother and Daughter

CHAPTER TEN

THE HIDDEN KNOWLEDGE

"Let the wise man, though he knows the truth,
behave among humanity as if he were an iodiot."
                    --Rhuddlwm Gawr

We were walking along the north path as Sarah spoke:
"There is certain hidden knowledge that has been entrusted to Y Tylwyth Teg--this is the knowledge of the wand
and the cup, the rood and the rosy cross. This is both the
lost word of the Masons and the lost knowledge of the
Rosicrucians.

"One learns of the alchemical marriage of the two
streams of force in the cup which, when transformed, is
consumed. This communion is with the God/dess and is a
preliminary invocation and a binding of the forces of the
elements. This is the magical link through which the Divine
presence begins to manifest itself. This is the actual union,
and is the key to the future progress of humanity. This is
the 'Great Work' which eats itself up, accomplishes its own
aims, nourishes the seeker, leaves no seed, and is perfect
unto himself; 'Redemption is the Goal of the Great Work.'"

"What kind of redemption are you talking about? Something like Christian redemption?" I asked suspiciously.

"No, redemption is really as simple as it appears complex. Although the veils of truth are obscure and many,
the truth itself is plain and of one substance. But truth
can only be reached through its veils.

"Redemption is a surrender and a rebirth."

"I listened intently as she continued:

"Rhuddlwm, in general, we consider the lower three
planes of human awareness as but a nursery school of learning.

133

This learning results in an eventual elevation of the consciousness above these planes. But the 'enlightened ones' always return to give assistance to others who are still entwined in the illusionary material world." She spoke with sparkling eyes, allowing time for me to understand and experience a spiritual moment of suspension.

I listened intently as she continued:

"Buddha and Christ both ascribed little importance to miracles, yet Christ performed mircales and Buddha forbade them. The message was the same--miracles and other psychic phenomena are an aspect of the physical world, and not the spiritual world. They are signposts which, although occurring along the path to enlightenment, are not goals within themselves.

"Psychic power and so called occult powers are but minor extensions of human capacity in the immediate material world. Although discipline and hard work are required to obtain psychic powers, you should not be concerned only with obtaining these powers, for you would be like an individual whose only goal is amassing great wealth. You would have power but without the capability of using it correctly, would not be able to cultivate spiritual values."

I pondered this as she paused.

"But if I did cultivate spiritual values along with the wealth, wouldn't that be a good thing?" I asked hesitantly.

"Yes, except that it is almost impossible to simultaneously acquire wealth and spirituality. The values are at odds. That is not to say that it could never happen, but it is highly unlikely. Many people have acquired positive values early in life, and utilized these values in their quest for personal success. But massive wealth in the past was acquired at the expense of others, precluding any spiritual advancement."

134

"Sarah, I disagree. I know people who have wealth and are seekers like I am."

"Rhuddlwm, was the wealth given to them or did they work for it?"

"Well. . .," I hesitated, "their parents are wealthy and this gives them security, but they don't act rich or anything like that. But I guess you are right—some of them reject the wealth from their parents because they didn't earn it. I don't know—I guess I'm confused. I like the idea of having money and buying the things that would make it easier to live, but I'm not that aggressive anymore. I'm not ambitious for money, I'm ambitious for knowledge. I wouldn't reject a million dollars, but I don't attach a great deal of importance to the idea of it anymore."

"Rhuddlwm, what would you do with a million dollars if you had it?"

I thought for what must have been a long time.

"Given my present level of knowledge, I think I would do a lot of teaching and visit those places which mean a great deal to me religiously and spiritually." I paused for a moment. "After that, I don't know. I guess maybe I would purchase some land where I would build a community where people who were seekers like I am could come and study."

She looked at me thoughtfully.

"Rhuddlwm, maybe there's hope for you yet." She smiled, her eyes twinkling. "Now we'd better get back."

Later that day, as we all sat under the trees in the oak grove, each of us were lost in thought. We had experienced the adoption rite, and each of us wore the symbol of our expected status—acorns made into a necklace.

Sarah spoke:

"Seekers, between the perfection of the Great Spirit and the imperfection of Humanity stand the Elemental Spirits.

"To spiritually aware people, the earth is peopled by a multitude of nature beings. They inhabit the forests and

135

mountains, trees and lakes, flowers and meadows. There are
four classifications of these nature beings.

"Fairies and sylphs, which are a creation of the air
realm, can be found above the earth's countryside ruling
the winds and the clouds.

"Gnomes, pixies, dryads, and wood nymphs are earth
spirits developed through the emanations of the earth.

"Water sprites, naiads, and water nymphs inhabit the
aquatic area of the earth.

"Salamanders, which are the residents of the fire
kingdom, have the least association with men.

"Unseen by physical sight, the earth elementals and
spirits are custodians of the earth's growth; minerals, vegetables, forests, valleys, and mountain strongholds are super-
vised by them."

"But how about the upper planes?" I asked.

"There are several classifications of spirits in the
evolution of the Spirit Realm on the upper plains," she
answered.

"First, the Seraphim, dedicating its invocation to
the Great Spirit, contemplates love on the Celestial plane.

"The Cherubim contemplates the wisdom of the Great
Spirit and emanates that wisdom on the Duality plane.

"Thrones administer the Divine Judgment of the Great
Spirit and form a powerful spiritual attraction which will
eventually lead every pilgrim in every realm back to a oneness with the eternal Great Spirit. They exist on the
spiritual plane.

"Dominions are administrators of the will of the Thrones
and are symbolized by the flaming sword on the Mental plane.

"Virtues execute the will of the Dominions and perform
all acts of miraculous healing on the Astral plane.

"Powers regulate the activities of spiritual purposes
on the Etheric plane.

"And finally, Principalities have authority over nations, governments, leaders, and world servers. They empower nations to carry out the Divine Plan and effect the Physical plane."

"But who are the watchers?" I asked.

"The four watchers are rulers over the four elemental kingdoms.

"The first, Michael, is a representative of the Powers and carries a sword, symbolic of fire. He is being clad in white and holds a pair of scales. This being represents the South.

"Gabriel wears a lily, symbolic of water, and an olive branch and carries a torch, symbolic of the great world. This being rules the West.

"Raphael is the trustee of creative talents and healing. The symbols are the staff, a lyre, and hands outstretched in healing. This being represents Earth and the East.

"Uriel is associated with musical arts and is a teacher of humanity. This being represents air and the North.

"The spirits which we are most likely to contact are the Guardians. Every human being is under the watchful eye of a group of guardian beings, but it is not until we yearn for spiritual growth that we attract a single Guardian or Spirit Guide. This being becomes the seeker's teacher and initiator through many ordeals until spiritual maturity has been achieved.

"As one progresses from seeker to master, more will be learned of the spirit world and it's inhabitants. It is through contact with these beings and their power that we ourselves attain spiritual development.

"It is also our duty to develop ourselves physically and become in tune with the spiritual polarity of opposites. This reflects as the sexual attraction of Humankind.

"You have all wondered what part sex plays in our religion. Human sex is the physical expression, the embodiment and incarnation of love. It can also serve a social

137

function, but first and foremost it is an expression of feeling between two people.

"Each one of us is a human being before being a man or a woman. Therefore, women have a right to be treated as a human being and not as a 'mere woman.' She is a living being, with all the dignity and the potential of a whole person. All attitudes which limit the possibilities of women are false. Women have the right to demand respect and equality with men, and the same is true for men.

"Men must learn to accept the feminine balance within themselves before they can accept the feminine balance of nature. This balance is utilized in ritual sex.

"The first aim of ritual sex is the reintegration of opposite polarities within the seeker's body, resulting in an identification of the physical body with the spiritual and mystical body.

"Sexual union, with the right person at the right time, will open the way to cosmic awareness.

"The universe and everything within its sphere came into being through the union of opposites on a cosmic seal.

"Echoing this concept, when seekers approach the sexual mystery as a sacrament they attain the orgasm of a complete union, and their act becomes one with the Divine Creation of the Great Spirit.

"Sexual union is only a physical act unless another element is added--love. Sexual love is mature love, but in current society is distorted and treated as destructive love. This is not because of the sex act itself but because of a false attitude towards sex.

"The power of transforming your attitude is in your mind. Sexual love is beautiful, fulfilling, and divine. When we rid ourselves of bigoted thinking, sexual love becomes a hopeful reaching out for the positive.

"Sex is the cosmic union of opposites--the primordial energy from which arises everything in the universe. This

is the bipoles process of creation and is manifest throughout the universe.

"Everything in creation is divided into positive and
negative male and female.

"When a predominantly masculine electric personality
is brought into a field of a predominantly female magnetic
one, a reaction occurs and power is generated. This is the
same reaction that causes the earth to rotate and the crops
to grow. This reaction provides a channel for the odic
force, which encircles the earth plane polarizing the surrounding atmosphere.

"Through study of the sexual principles of Dewianath
Cymmry, seekers can achieve an extension of ecstatic sexual
climax for over an hour, resulting in complete relaxation
and rejuvenation. But, it is the ultimate destiny of the
soul to achieve completion through union of opposites within
a seeker's own body. This being is reborn on the higher
planes as a divine androgyne.

"The second aim of ritual sex is to utilize the etheric
odic energy of the aura to perform magick. This is done by
'raising the power' during the sexual act. The generation of
power is accomplished by each of the participants concentrating on sending out this energy to perform a specific action.

"The only danger in the use of ritual sex is not
thinking the right thoughts at the time of consumation. Let
the seeker beware."

"Should we treat sex magick as a secret?" I asked.

"Although the Sacred Knowledge is hidden, it is not
secret. Remember the saying--'Honor the secrets, reveal
them constantly.'"

"To acquire the knowledge, you must give up attachment
and desire. You must become one with the Force, the Great
Spirit. You must find yourself by understanding truth."

We sat bemused by these ideas dashing madly by as she
continued:

"Seekers, you are but yet children in a world of child-dren. You must become adults--so you will be able to teach the children how to grow up.

"Most seekers when they are just learning define things wrongly. They become so caught up in their own definitions that they cannot accept new concepts that disagree with old ones."

"What do you mean, Sarah?" asked a red haired girl.

"I have heard some of you talk about good karma and bad karma. This is not correct. There is no negative karma and there is no positive karma. There is only karma--the law--the Force. This Force is the beginning and the end of all."

We all leaned forward, completely engrossed in her words.

"To contact this universal Force, a person must respect himself and forgive himself for all signs, imagined or actual."

"How do you do that?"

"You must surrender your ego and start again for a new perspective. Everything is the Great Spirit--I am the Great Spirit. To realize this truth, you must listen to the still small voice within you--your Guide.

"All of you have gone on your Quest and, from reports, you have all experienced this voice in various ways. You, Rhuddlwm, saw your Guide as an old man who taught you ancient wisdom. Others of you experienced voices or visions and one of you even conjured a familiar. These are all valid.

"While you meditate, you can contact this point--this center within yourself and again experience the presence of your Guide.

"Quiet your mind, and disappear into your mantra. Choose a task to do, keeping your mind quiet. Become that task. If you are picking flowers, you are the flower. You are the earth, the sky, the hand that is doing the picking.

140

If you are with someone else, become that other person. Share yourself with them because you are them.

"You must give up striving to learn the key to the universe, because as soon as you do, the key will come to you.

"You must give up your ego in order to seek and progress on the path.

"Seekers, there are three ways of realizing the truth:

--through direct experience in meditation or personal enlightenment.

--through reasoning or inference by reading or watching others--observation.

--and, by trusting that there are truly special beings that have become enlightened. Trust is the most difficult way. But if you surrender to trust, you can gain eternal union with the light of understanding--the great god, Lugh.

"You must die and be reborn a new human, changed and perfected. You must experience sadness and despair, depression and loneliness beyond description.

"When I say that you must surrender your ego, I do not mean that you will lose it completely or permanently. But, your ego is changed; it joins with the Great Spirit and becomes one.

"Center yourself--forget about what you are getting out of life--live 'the way of the seeker.' 'The way' is the harmony of the universe; the dance of life, and you are the dancer.

"As the 'Story of Why' taught you, desire is not an evil thing, but it can be a trap. It is desire that sets Humankind on the path to seek.

"Do what you must do, but dedicate the fruits of your labor to the Great Spirit.

"You must be ready to experience enlightenment--no one is ever enlightened who is not ready. When you are ready, the Guide will be where you are."

I thought back to that day on Majorca.

"A teacher points the way--a Guide _is_ the way." Sarah looked at me and smiled. "But only the way to balance."

She continued:

"There are three basic methods of progression along the path to balance. They must _all_ be utilized in the search for harmony:

--Balance through knowledge, which is making the mind aware of your physical being.

--Balance through love. 'Thou art God/dess' sums up the theme for this step. But remember, that if you are God/dess, so is everyone else. God/dess is in everything. God/dess is love, but love by entering into deep involvement with everything.

--Balance through wisdom; to use reason to discover the point from which all things begin--The point at which the three rays of light emanate.

"Listen to the Story of Balance." She began:

"The Great Spirit, in True Freedom
Walked, full of compassion
In the deep and perfect way of wisdom.
Full of mercy, she
Leaned down
And saw only
Three moving structures
Of the seeking mind, and
That in their essence
They were empty.
And the Great One said:
O Cerridwen, Beloved Goddess,
Here, form is emptiness,
Emptiness is form.
Form is nothing other
Than emptiness.
Emptiness is nothing other

142

Than form.
Although there is form,
There is emptiness;
Although there is emptiness,
There is form.
It is the same
With sensations,
And perceptions,
And the preformed structures
Of consciousness.
O Cernunnos, deal disciples,
Here, all qualities
Have the character
Of emptiness.
They have neither birth
Nor death;
They are neither
Defiled nor pure;
Neither incomplete nor complete.
Therefore,
Dear disciples;
Where there is emptiness
There is
Neither form
Nor sensation
Nor perception
Nor preformed structures,
Nor consciousness.
Neither eye nor ear
Nor nose, nor tongue
Nor body nor thought
Neither form, nor sound
Nor smell, nor taste
Nor touch
Nor object of thought.

Nor field of vision
Nor even an object
Of consciousness.
Neither knowledge
Nor ignorance
Nor even
Decline and death
Nor disappearance
Of decline and death
Neither suffering
Nor creation
Nor   end
Nor way
Nor knowledge
Nor gift
Nor refusal of a gift
Nor obtaining
Nor not obtaining.
Therefore,
O Rhiannon,
Because of it's detachment
Because of it's confidence
In perfect wisdom
The Great Spirit
Does not know
Anxious thoughts.
It does not tremble.
Consoled by what
Is not oblivion
It has overcome
What might have
Threatened it with death
All those who appear
As   Guides
in the Five periods
Of time.

Trusting
In perfect wisdom
Awakened
Clearheaded,
To the supreme, just and perfect light.
Perfect wisdom
Must therefore be known.
This is the great song of knowledge,
The incomparable song,
The unmatched song,
The consoler of all suffering,
The song of truth,
Without error.
This unsurpassable song,
Is the incantation of Great Wisdom
What is said thus,
'Go, go, go beyond,
Go all together,
Beyond the beyond
Where lies the way of Gwlad Yr Hav
Which is the Wisdom of the Great Spirit.'"

We sat entranced as she finished. What a strange story! It seemed to reveal a mystery to us, but we were only catching a glimpse of it.

"You have all studied the kabbalah, you walked the path of the Sufi, you have dwelt in the forest with Pan, and discovered the forces of Mother Nature. You have all realized by now that there is no Hidden Knowledge; that there are no forbidden secrets, only mysteries and these cannot be explained, only revealed.

"We of Y Tylwyth Teg have chosen each one of you to fulfill a prophecy made over a thousand years ago when the last of the ancient ones were being persecuted by the Christians: 'We will again reveal the Hidden Knowledge, but only when a thousand years have passed, when it will again be safe to walk the sacred path to the oak grove. Only then will the apple tree be the tree of knowledge. Only then will it again be safe.'"

We listened as she continued:

"Each of you here was born on a certain date in a certain sign which is very important to your religion. Each of you represent a sacred festival. But much more than that, you are each a part of the wheel; the wheel of Balance, the wheel of life, and the wheel of the year.

"You will go from here in a few more months back to your separate countries and back to your everyday lives. But remember this: Be in the world but not of the world. Teach others as you have been taught. Keep the knowledge hidden from those who would seek it out. You are children of the Goddess and keepers of the flame--you will be needed in years to come--Be ready!"

She paused for a few moments, as if to receive support from the elements.

"Seekers, we are a Spiritual Order dedicated to an attunement with nature through Psychic Development and Inner Awareness Training using the Ancient Celtic Mystic Techniques of RELINKING.

"You are RELINKING with each other, male and female, understanding so that you are no longer alone, but can touch each other without fear.

"You are RELINKING with the flow of Nature, with Earth, Sky, and Running Water, so that you may walk in balance with the Earth Mother and Great Spirit." She paused.

"Humankind in its ignorance has always assumed that the Earth would rejuvenate Herself, no matter what it did. But the Earth can lose her resiliency. Her waters are polluted, Her soil is becoming dust, Her forests are destroyed. Someday She may be beyond Her ability to heal Herself. But what we do to Her, we do to ourselves.

146

"When Humankind and nature are in harmony, the Earth is a happy place. There is great strength in this idea which is the Basic Foundation of our Religious Teachings.

"You must call the Earth your Mother, you must protect Her and learn to live in harmony with Her. You must learn Her moods and rhythms. You must love the Earth--from Her you are born, of Her sustenance you do eat, and to Her you will return.

"Your world must be a Circle of beauty and freedom, of innocence, learning neither guilt nor shame. To you all things of Nature, all acts of gentleness, love, and pleasure must be sacred.

"Although what we do is in essence religious, we are not long-faced mystics forbidding all pleasure with a promise of eternal bliss, as you discovered." We all laughed.

"Rather, we approach our works with a spontaneous joy and the playfulness of a butterfly.

"Natural concepts which are important to us are: Non-sexism, mind-body interaction, centering, harmony of the spirit, balance, gentleness,and deprogramming.

"Yes, we, the Children of the Earth, are also the Children of the Morning Star; we seek only to dance the dance of joy, the celebration of life."

As Sarah completed her talk, we were all silent and lost in thought. The chief Elders who had been listening throughout it all, now spoke:

"We of Dynion Mwyn are creating and establishing an international working community, founded on the principle of universal truth and teaching the spiritual concept of RELINKING.

"In this process, we have helped you to get your hands together, through RELINKING with yourselves, others, and Nature. This was done through your class and workshop interactions.

"We have established this school of esoteric spiritual teachings which provides practical knowledge of survival

147

and religious instruction for our community and your rebirth
into today's world.

"Y Tylwyth Teg taught you NOT by forcing spiritual
knowledge and preconceived ideas down your throat, but by
helping each of you to become aware of your own capabilities
and potentials.

"In our religious order, Nature is our God/dess. We
see her in all things, for Nature and Spirit are linked.
Without this connection there is disharmony and inbalance.

"Seekers, we are of the Old Religion and teaching the
ancient knowledge. We are RELINKING you with others and with
nature. We are also helping you develop an inner awareness
of your spiritual heritage which will transform your consciousness into a new dimension of reality. You will become
the teachers of the New Age.

"Come, seekers, join us in celebration of an Old
Religion for the New Age! Welcome, Seekers! Welcome to
the beautiful family!"

We were being told of our acceptance as members! We
all leaped up and slapped each other on the back and hugged
each other. We had done it! Each following his or her
own path, each in his or her own way, but we had made it!
We would never be the same!

The Elder was smiling broadly and Sarah was looking
wistfully at me with tears in her eyes. No, we would never
be the same.

149

CHAPTER ELEVEN

CYMMRY NATURE MAGICK AND HEALING

"A begger went to a door, asking for something to
be given to him. The owner answered, and said,
'I am sorry, but there is nobody here.' 'I don't
want anybody,' said the begger, 'I want food.'"
                    --Rhuddlwm Gawr

One of the questions that had long haunted me involved
magick and healing. So much superstition, so much power, so
much conflict had been strewn about this emotional battle-
field. I also sensed that most people of past ages, out of
ignorance, never quite understood what magick was.

This conflict unleashed through the centuries was
partly explained by our teacher as she took us over some of
the rough waters of History with the gentle wisdom of a sea
captain knowing the shifting tides and currents. Her eyes,
cool and steady in dark green shadows, had glints of light
in them. It was like looking into a clear mountain stream
and catching flashes from the bright pebbles.

"The underlying tradition of magick is a vital part
of the human experience all over the world. Paradise,
Atlantis, the Flood, the cataclysm, all dessribe the same
'Force,'" she began.

"All magick really means is the control of events in
accordance with inner will. One of the great teachers,
Jesus, used this inner power to perform healing miracles.
He has developed a control over natural forces which few
mortals have since accomplished. He understood the very
nature of life itself.

"A Cymmry Gwiddion does the same thing. He or she is
able to contact the forces of nature and live harmoniously
with the Great Spirit. We use what is natural to us in our
environment, instead of creating false conditions.

150

"Natural magick is an ability to live in the world of naked reality instead of the dark nightmare of personal illusion. Natural magick also reveals the ability to deal with people and forces as they really are, and not as they appear to be.

"A natural magician visualizes his or her desires in accordance to natural laws, and not for selfish ends."

This description altered my idea of the meaning of control and both frightened and fascinated me. The image I was developing was one of natural integration with the course of the universe; an elevation of perception and energy levels as a result of awareness--an outflowing of energy rather than a grasping for it. I feared the image of spider webs and demons sprouting from victims.

"Magick masters time and space. Magick is everywhere. It is the wonderous force that creates a flower and lets us enjoy its beauty. It is the power behind the growth of every leaf and tree, the creation of every mountain and stream. These are the outer symbols of the inner world. To control this power, we must have the sensitivity and patience to sense the great harmony that exists in the universe, and to see the spirits within the elements of earth, water, fire, and air. These spirits will willingly help us if we just ask them.

"Everything is alive around us and can be contacted-- the stones, the earth, the trees, and the animals. If we communicate with these elemental forces, they will respond in a positive manner. Elementals respond instantly if loving thoughts are sent their way.

"To understand what it is to become a Gwiddion, a natural magician, you must not only study and understand the universe, but also learn to link with it. When relinking with Nature becomes more important than your own personal ego, then all doubts, fears, and worries will fall away and a sense of love and peace will become a part of your entire being. The

151

structure of your body will become lighter and the texture of your skin will change."

I was wondering now if there were steps to take in learning to merge with our inner self. The teacher spoke softly and easily as if to answer my thoughts.

"When we do not limit ourselves to our physical body, we can expand infinitely and touch the heavens. We can even experience the reality of planets and galaxies. To feel and become at one with Nature, one does not need complex tools. You can start with a rock. Learn to sense the rock's spirit by handling it and feeling it constantly. You will make contact with it eventually. Also, contact trees. They are soothing and like to be acknowledged. Every tree is capable of giving off wonderful healing energies. However, some harbor bad spirits. Therefore, before approaching a tree to receive healing energy, it is necessary to find out if it is safe.

"The best way to find out is to walk around with your palms facing towards the tree. You will gradually begin to detect the different forms of energy that trees radiate. You will feel in harmony with some of them and you will reject others. Trust your instincts.

"Practice regularly. Everything in the universe gives off phychic vibrations, and it is possible to 'feel' the vibrations of every living thing. One should, therefore, take a walk at least once a day in order to 'feel' the trees, flowers, and stones. It is also possible to 'hear' with the body.

"The left side of the body reacts differently than the right side does. Therefore, the sensitivity in the left hand is different from the sensitivity in the right. The right side is the giving side, and the left side is the receiving."

It was incredible to think of our bodies as such sensitive instruments. It really allowed a new perception to develop about how we interact in natural space and with

152

natural objects. Our teacher herself was setting up energy fields of powerful force--I could sense barriers falling, and continual openings of new channels. It was like seeing the tide come in, the many rivulets pouring along the open bay, seeking the upper beaches.

"Nature is a law unto herself and a person alone is pitifully small in comparison with the gigantic forces of the universe. The seasons occur year after year, and nothing can reverse them. Nature gives birth but also causes death. Her creative aspects are balanced by her destructive qualities.

"Societies like those of Atlantis have been based completely on her natural laws but have suffered devastation in order to bring about an even more advanced form of creation. For nothing is every lost--it just appears to be."

This seemed a bit of a cold write-off to an old civilization. A sense of loss hammered at me. It made me feel so small that the world I knew might be destroyed so easily. Then other feelings of curiosity swept over me again.

Our teacher glanced over us warmly. Her eyes focused on a tree near the window as she began to expand her arms and introduce the area of natural healing. Her hands reached out, supporting her words and underlying the basic truths of the Craft; her palms flowed easily along the surface of air currents showing the degree of relationships she held to natural pathways of energy flow.

"The dualistic concept of all creation is deeply ingrained in each of Y Tylwyth Teg: action--reaction, male-- female, God--Goddess, above--below, and so on. It is from the interaction of these opposites, and the balance resulting from the tension of conflicting pulls of force, that causes creative energies to flow. Equilibrium is a harmonious balance of all opposites in which lies a potential flow of vital energies. When these energies flow, they seek to reestablish balance. For example, throughout the cycle of seasons of the year, the God and Goddess are seeking balance.

153

It is this control over balance and imbalance, equilibrium and flow, that allows you to direct the flow of vital healing energies.

"Energy is composed of opposites: in--out, up--down, etc. Although we divide them to talk about them, these opposites within energy can never be separated. One cannot exist without the other. Positive and negative attractions are both necessary for movement. Together, they create vibrations. When the opposites are in correct relationship, the result is balance. Balance is a state of completeness. If you have a need and it is filled, you are satisfied--you are complete.

"The second thing we can say about energy is that it is seeking a balance. Balance is the essence of health and life. Seeking a balance is the natural state of the universe.

"Persons who are at peace with themselves project a positive aura into their environment and, by attunement, share energy with others. There are three basic concepts of attunement. The first is the co-existence of plants, animals, and humans, and their support for one another. The second is that each level of life has its own language, and the third is that humankind can communicate with Nature directly by learning its language.

"Because 'held energy' is an incomplete form of 'the Word'--the Great Spirit--there is essentially a separation and an imbalance within the person. 'Held energies' occupy identifiable physical territories--the sadness located near your heart, the fear in your guts. These areas that hold energy disturb the natural flow of body energy.

"When 'held energy' occupies an area of the physical body, no other energy may pass through, and your body's capacity for channeling energy is reduced. This held energy can manifest itself as a quality of physical weight and a person may feel emotionally 'heavy.'"

154

I recognized this sensation of held energy. As it was described, it can be held because of injury or disease, or even strangely enough because the person desires it. It is peculiar that humans seek uncomfortable sensations at times, and the held energy is a feeling that is not always pleasant. Most of us are used to it; in fact, it is part of our personal reality. Apparently, our egos are actually afraid of losing that feeling, and perceive a loss of self if the feeling is lost.

Incredibly our egos perceive a void if the held energies, however negative, are lost. Fear of total emptiness is perhaps more intense than the unpleasantness of the held energy.

We are cautioned that before healing ourselves, we would need to empty ourselves of this held energy by taking responsibility for our own feelings--admitting that we like being unhappy, disappointed, angry, and sad. Otherwise, we wouldn't be that way.

It was calming to know that we have the power to change those feelings--that we can remain the way we are or choose to become one with the energy flow of nature.

After discharging this energy, we must watch out for old habits; our response patterns of anger and fear. Indulging in emotions that create separation while trying to heal others is fruitless. We must allow the life force of nature to move within us.

Our teacher continued, pulling in many new aspects of psychic healing which unified much of the knowledge we had already accumulated. It had a strong effect on me.

"Psychic healing can be a communication and a sharing between two humans. But before you can begin healing others, you must know your own body by relinking your consciousness to your subconscious. You must be able to touch yourself. This is done through meditation techniques and exercises described earlier.

155

"Energy is the source of all life. Yet, humans interrupt the flow within themselves by isolating portions of the total energy, creating an imbalance. Once you have experienced healing within yourself, you will understand how it happens to the person you are healing. But, it is also important to realize that healing takes time, and since it occurs within the person on many different levels, you may not know whether you are touching them at the beginning of a healing cycle or at the end. If imbalances are encountered at the beginning of a healing cycle, it may appear that nothing is happening, but if they are touched at the moment of discharge, miracles can occur.

"When you first touch someone, you will begin to balance the forces around the person's body. You will renew that which is depleted, and cleanse away that which is negative, simply by being there.

"While you work, the psychic energy will direct you. It will tell you what to do. You don't have to think about what to do, just flow with the energy.

"You can never do anything to another person. But you can make energy available to someone and bring about a healing if they are willing to accept it. The responsibility of change rests with each individual. Therefore, you are free to give all the energy you wish. Most people will not take more than they can handle.

"There are three principles of psychic healing:
--Energy Transfer
--Structural Integration, and
--Psychic Reading

"The first principle of transferring energy supposes that if you give an individual life, love, and energy, they will use these to activate their inner Force and achieve freedom. Listen with your own psychic centers for the readiness of a place to discharge energy. Not all locations are equally active or inactive. Use both of your hands on the

156

body whenever and wherever possible. You are a battery.
Your right hand is positive and your left hand is negative.
Energy passes between them.

"Next, ground whatever energy comes from the individual,
as it may be harmful to you.

"As you touch the individual and take in held energy,
periodically remove your hands and shake them as if you were
shaking something out of them. This will get rid of held
energy which you might accumulate yourself."

I had always felt tuned in to so many of the destructive
types of energies and would flare up at the least suggestion
of negativity, sensing some powerful hostility. How useless
it was! I would allow myself to get into a snowballing effect
of anger and lose all control. All positive thoughts would be
useless even if my brain willed them. Grounding this would
be no less than a miracle!

"The second principle is structural integration. Held
energy can be released by correcting the body's structure.
This is done by using the principle of transference of energy
to help the muscles loosen and move the bones back into correct alignment.

"Structural displacement is a sign that an individual
has changed the physical organization of the body by keeping
his feelings inside, therefore trapping energy.

"Before attempting structural alignment, though, be
sure you are knowledgeable in the various procedures, for
improper manipulation could cause great harm.

"The third principle is psychic reading. This is a
special kind of feeling--Feeling how the body's energy is
flowing inside. During a psychic reading, this knowledge
takes on form, pattern, and dimension which are visual
qualities.

"We see with our inner self, or Third Eye, but feel with
the facility of our solar plexus. A healthy body is 'seen'
emanating an inner radiance which is balanced. An unhealthy

157

body has dark places and breaks within the aura. Through psychic reading, you can detect problems in the energy flow, allowing you to make the corrections that are necessary.

"Through psychic reading you also allow yourself to sense the qualities of energy that are locked inside a person's subconscious, thereby discovering the ways in which the person has defined or limited him/her self. To identify the meaning of a 'held energy' is the ultimate purpose of psychic reading.

"Using your psychic ability for healing and relinking requires sensitivity, tact, and love. Because of the extraordinary importance of psychic healing as part of Y Tylwyth Teg philosophy, it is taught only by a guide to the individual seeker in his quest for universal truth."

The trouble with these series of insights was that they gave me a vision of wholeness and positive flows of energy, but I had barely begun the process of integrating with nature. I could look back now and see how much I had learned, but by looking ahead see how far I had to go.

Perhaps these feelings were a necessary plateau of learning that I had reached. Somehow I would have to pull myself together and practice the art of knowing and feeling nature, and eventually master the healing arts themselves. I knew one thing: The idea of healing people attracted me very much!

CHAPTER TWELVE

THE SECRET KEYS

"Once knowledge has been translated into the printed
word, it has a life of its own. The Teacher can
no longer control how knowledge should be used,
nor who shall receive it. Accidents may occur
which would take the knowledge out of the hands
of the teacher and place it into the hands of an
overeager student, an irreverent materialist, a
shallow person greedy for power, a stranger
possessing more curiosity than is good for him
or an illiterate who destroys it or carelessly
passes it on."--Edward Albertson

Our teacher was discussing Reincarnation:
"Humankind in its essential spiritual nature is a seed
of the Great Spirit, and this seed is 'planted' in the phyical
and etheric worlds in order that it may develop to the highest
possible degree. In the human kingdom of nature, the individual who has reached this state is known as an adept, or
perfect human," she said looking at me.

"I thought that was one of our flaws--trying for the
perfect state, or at least believing we might be there."

"Well, you're right. Such an achievement is not possible
in any one lifetime since there is neither time nor opportunity in which to fully develop every human power. Therefore, every human has an ego which enters into a physical
incarnation at birth and withdraws from it at death. During
each occasion, various physical conditions, environments, and
activities are experienced so that progress is made in each
life. We gradually progress until all necessary learning
experiences are gained and all weaknesses overcome."

"Cromlch"

"You believe that? That all weaknesses can be overcome?"

"Yes. By this means, humankind is assured of ultimate success. Each cycle on the ascending spiral path by which humankind reaches its goal of adeptship consists of a descent of a portion of the power, life, and consciousness of the ego into physical incarnation and a subsequent return to a higher position on the spiral."

"Higher position on the spiral?"

"Each new cycle opens as a result of a change of consciosness experienced by the ego at a certain period after the conclusion of the preceding cycle. We see this change as the result of a thirst for further growth and fuller self-expression. Knowing that these can only be gained by re-entry into physical life, the ego, which abides on the astral plane, turns its attention to the physical world. Does this make sense?"

"I think so. Keep going."

"A force of ego power is projected to the etheric plane, where the mental body is formed."

"Egoic power?"

"Yes. The ego force that penetrates into the realm of of the physical plane where a body of emotional desire is formed. Finally, the ego force attaches itself to the first cell formed by the sperm and egg, which later grows into the physical body.

"During each life, the mental, emotional, and physical bodies develop and the ego becomes increasingly conscious of them. This process of growth through physical experiences continues until death, the moment and manner of which are governed by the law of cause and effect. The physical body is then laid aside and the process of return begun."

We had slowed somewhat as we walked. I was thinking that this explained a great deal of what was really occurring. Sarah leaped ahead of me.

162

"For a time, the length of which depends upon the nature
and strength of the emotional life while on earth, the ego
is conscious in the emotional body and continues to reap
karma at that level. Valuable lessons are learned, evolution-
ary progress is made and eventually the etheric body is laid
aside and the last stage of the return journey is completed.
This consists of life on the astral plane, a state corres-
ponding to paradise; that is, Gwald Yr Hav--the Summerplace."

"Is that the final resting place?"

"No. Eventually, when the higher egos have found their
fullest possible mental expression, they leave the astral
plane and rise to the mental plane, where they become masters."

"Do we keep the same sex when we incarnate?" I asked.

"No," replied Sarah, "you may change sexual characteristics or you may be the same sex in your next life. That
depends on your karma."

"But does karmic law really determine who I will be in
my next life?" I asked.

Sarah paused a moment in order to collect her thoughts,
smoothly assessed my face for wrinkles of skepticism, and
then continued.

"Karma is the doctrine of the law of cause and effect.
Under karmic law, every human action, whether mental, emotional, or physical, produces an appropriate reaction. These
reactions are not always received in the same life in which
the act takes place. They occur only when conditions arise
in which they can be justly and appropriately experienced.
The operation of the law of cause and effect demands that
causes must produce their effects at the level, on the plane,
and in the world in which the cause was generated. Physical
actions produce physical effects. Emotional, mental, and
spiritual actions produce their effects in their appropriate
worlds. Since every phyical action of one life cannot
produce its full reaction during that lifetime, a return to

163

earth is necessitated in order that the essential conditions, namely awareness in a physical body, can be established. Each person generates the cause of which his or her later experiences are the effects."

"What phenomenal computer system could keep track of all of us? It's hard to reason out," I commented.

"Our human flaws deny us the insights and understanding at times to see the whole picture. Conditions of human life, whether of health, happiness, capacity and opportunity, or of desires, sorrow, weaknesses, and lamentation, are the results of the operation of exact law. Thus, the doctrine of reincarnation and karma provide the only possible solution of the problem of human birth and opportunity with logic and justice. The difference in bodily and mental capacity, and the environment into which a human is born are the direct results of his or her conduct in this or a previous life."

"It is a logical solution, but isn't that too neat a view?" I asked.

"Think of this--Karma neither punishes nor rewards, but it is the universal law which guides events in such a way that eventually harmony between cause and effect is fully reestablished. It is not subjective, then, like the cycle of water from the ocean through the rainfall and return to the ocean. It is more complex than a series of events, but this law of reincarnation and karma does provide a logical philosophy of life which can be stated in the following postulates:

"Perfection is the destiny of the spiritual self of every human.

"Reincarnation provides the necessary time and opportunity for self-perfection.

"The law of action and reaction insures justice to all humankind.

"The attainment of perfection is rendered possible by the presence of a divine power at work within the spiritual self of every human being."

164

"Sarah, how does Astrology relate to karma and reincarnation?"

"Rhuddlwm, Astrology is a spiritual science that in-
volves the relationship between the macrocosm and the micro-
cosm. The horoscope is the blueprint which illustrates this
relationship as a pattern of energy fields.

"When you chose your body, it is made clear to you which
qualities are needed in order to learn a particular lesson.

"The Horoscope Chart is a blueprint of our karmic balance
and it is also a portrait of those qualities which make up
your character."

"That's a bit scary!"

"It is a little frightening, but always remember, the
stars can impel, but they cannot compel. Astrology can map
the influences operating on your personality through symbols,
but that doesn't mean you will automatically give in to them."

"Like a weather map?" I asked. "I can calculate the
possibility of thunderstorms, but it depends on where the
weather fronts converge."

"Yes, Rhuddlwm, I understand what you are saying. The
Signs of the Zodiac are symbols of great and potent forces.
Their position at specific points on the Zodiac can be a
beneficial or a deterring influence. Also, your horoscope
indicates what conditions you will encounter throughout your
life. It does not tell you what will happen, only what is
likely to happen. Astrology is one of the tools used in
discovery of your true self."

"Could you explain more about astrology and how it works?"

"In Astrology there are four factors which must be
dealth with: Planets, Signs, Houses, and Aspects. Planets
are the energies which are operating. Signs represent how
the energies operate. As the planets pass through the Signs,
the energies are conditioned, which shows an individual's
capacity and ability to achieve what the Planets indicate.

The Houses show where the energies will work and indicate
the opportunities offered by your environment, while the
Aspects illustrate the flow of forces between the Planets,
and show how you use or abuse the energies operating in your
magnetic field."

"What about the birth signs?" I questioned.

"The Zodiac is divided into three-hundred sixty degrees,
with each Sign having thirty degrees." She arranged some
sticks on the ground to illustrate the Zodiac.

"Aries is on the first house in a natural Zodiac, with
Taurus on the second and the rest of the signs in succession.
Each sign has a planetary ruler and some planets rule two
signs." She motioned toward the ground with her hand.

"This sign is Aries. It is ruled by Mars and is a
cardinal, Fire sign. It's positive and masculine, the untamed
fire of impulse. In the physical world it rules the head.
This sign influences the days between March twenty-second
and April twenty-first.

"Here is Taurus, ruled by Venus. It's a fixed, Earth
sign; a Feminine and receptive sign of the freshly plowed
Earth of Springtime ready for seed. In the physical body it
rules the throat and back of the brain. It's dates include
April twenty-second to May twenty-first.

"Gemini is this one and is ruled by Mercury. It is mutable, and an Air sign, neutral in expression; here today and
gone tomorrow. The twins rule the nervous system, the hands,
the shoulders, the arms, and the lungs. It influences May
twenty-second to June twenty-first.

"Cancer is over here." Her hand smoothed the dirt. "It
is ruled by the Moon, is Cardinal and a Water sign. It is
feminine and receptive. It represents the surging and ebbing
of emotions. Cancer rules the heart, the breasts, the stomach,
and the solar plexis. It's influence comes between June
twenty-second and July twenty-first.

166

"Leo is ruled by the Sun. It's a fixed, Fire sign, the steady, controlled fire of affection. It governs the heart and the spine, and shows it's strength between July twenty-second and August twenty-first.

"Virgo is next, ruled by Mercury. It is mutable, an Earth sign, feminine, and receptive. It represents the time of reaping and assimilation, and governs the intestinal tract. It's influence spans August twenty-second to September twenty-first.

"Libra is ruled by Venus. It is Cardinal and an Air sign. It's characteristics are positive and masculine. It's emblem is the balance. It rules the kidneys and it's influences occur September twenty-second to October twenty-first.

"Scorpio, here, is ruled by Mars and Pluto. It's a fixed, Water sign. Scorpio is feminine, receptive, and signifies creativity. It rules the generative system and the rectum. It dominates October twenty-second to November twenty-first.

"This is Sagittarius, ruled by Jupiter. It is a mutable, Fire sign; positive and masculine. It represents the fire of the spirit and rules the hips and thighs. It has a great deal to do with arterial blood. It's time is November twenty-second to December twenty-first.

"Capricorn is ruled by Saturn and is a cardinal, Earth sign. Capricorn is feminine and receptive. It's characteristic mood is 'climbing to the highest peaks.' It rules the knees and the bony structure of the body. It's position is December twenty-second to January twenty-first.

"This is Aquarius, my sign. It is ruled by Saturn and Uranus. It is a fixed, Air sign and is positive and masculine. Aquarius is represented by the crystal clear air of winter. It rules the circulatory system and the ankles. It's dates are January twenty-second to February twenty-first.

167

"The last is Pisces, ruled by Neptune and Jupiter. It is mutable, a Water sign, and is feminine and receptive. It represents the fish is ceaseless motion. Pisces rules the feet and influences the time from February twenty-second to March twenty-first."

"What is the importance of all this?" I asked in confusion.

Sarah smiled patiently. "Studying the signs and planets is very important. The more knowledge you have of the meaning of the planets and signs, the greater will be your ability to interpret a Horoscope Chart correctly, thus establishing the relationship between you and the Cosmos.

"Rhuddlwm, the unity of Y Tylwyth Teg, and of the path, is a fact. The connection between the ancient practical philosophy and the present ones are based upon the higher level unity of knowledge. We are here to give higher knowledge—Not to teach what people pretend that they already know! For, a person's refinement is the goal at which the inner teachings of our way aim. In order to accomplish this, there is always a tradition handed down by a living chain of adepts, who select candidates to whom to impart this knowledge.

"The methods of our teachings are valid to three types of people:

--To those attracted by techniques and who seek ordinary psychological stimuli;

--To those wishing knowledge of the various types of religions and philosophies;

--And for individuals and groups interested in developing enlightenment as correctly prescribed by a guide.

"We seek people unconcerned about externals, and thus are able to keep pure our capacity to continue the path.

"Our path derives its substance in unbroken succession from the earliest times. It maintains its connection, in a parallel way, with both the ancients and the contemporary teachers by direct communications of being.

168

"It is important to remember two things: Speak to everyone in accordance with his or her understanding, and the task of the teacher is to teach.

"Let me tell you a story:"

* * * * *

"Once upon a time there was a seeker. As she was sitting in contemplation, she noticed that the devil was also sitting near her. The seeker asked, 'Why are you sitting there making no mischief?'

"The devil raised his head wearily and replied, 'Since the Christian ministers and other would-be teachers of the path have increased in such numbers, there is nothing left for me to do.'"

* * * * *

"That story shows how our search for truth can sometimes become sidetracked by dogma and prejudice."

"But, Sarah, what about the 'Secret Knowledge' I'm always hearing about?"

"In all mystical philosophy, in every religion, a great deal is hidden from the profane. There are two reasons for this: To keep knowledge from the unworthy--'Do not cast pearls before swine'--and to cause the seekers to exercise their minds in searching for knowledge--'He who has eyes, let him see. He who has ears, let him hear.'

"Y Tylwyth Teg uses several methods in transmitting 'Hidden Knowledge.' One of these is the development of techniques and procedures which will aid the seeker in contacting his or her latent inner strengths, such as meditation and exercise.

"We also use sounds, visions, and other sensory stimuli in consciousness raising like dancing, chanting, etc.

"We organize local groves of seekers composed of people chosen because of their harmonizing influence on each other. These are our study groups.

169

"We teach that by working together, seekers may liberate a dynamic flow of energy which will aid in their progression along the path.

"Legends, triads, and parables are taught which establish new patterns that will help the mind operate in a manner which will aid in psychic development.

"Working communities are created by selecting those groves who are the most oriented toward Balance, and bringing them into contact with others.

"And finally, our teachers select techniques and procedures based on their workability within the cultures they encounter."

Sarah and I began to discuss the Mystic Keys, those various instruments to man's enlightenment. Many have been prominent over the centuries and come in different forms: Ancient holy books such as the Bible, the Koran, the Torah, and the Tarot. We explored how these keys come through symbolic revelation in dreams and meditation, through esoteric instruction of our spiritual guide, and even in one's awareness of the relationship to his surroundings.

"In a sacred work, Sarah, would a particular historical event qualify as a Key?"

"Yes, in a holy book or ancient legend, such an event may be instead, a subjective experience of a race or nation or individual. You might say that each of the heroes of a story represent a condition of consciousness and a quality of character, so we come to the point that each story may be regarded as a graphic description of the experiences of the soul in it's journey through stages of enlightenment to it's goal of merging with the universal consciousness. While some keys can always be seen in universal terms in many religions, others are specific symbols revealed to seekers of Y Tylwyth Teg as a way to enlightenment. Each physical object and certain words carry such symbolic meanings."

"Are you referring to the elements?" I asked.

"Yes," Sarah replied. "Do you remember their symbolic import?"

170

I hesitated for only a moment. "I think so. 'Earth'
pertains to the waking state; 'Water' pertains to the
emotions, 'Air' pertains to intuition, and 'Fire' pertains
to the mind. That reminds me--I was gong to ask you about
the Tarot. Isn't it supposed to be a revelation of arcane
wisdom, hidden within symbolism?"

"I'll tell you about that later because the symbols are
covering the walls of the room in the main study. Let's
walk back."

Colder now, shadows breaking and shifting in waves on
the rolling hills, we retraced the snow trail leaving larger
boot marks in continuous winding lines across this lonely
landscape. Refreshed, filled with thoughts, I hurried back
toward the farmhouses, curious about another set of mystic
symbols. Tightening her scarf, Sarah led the way.

Back at the community building, after the midday meal
and work, Sarah and I resumed our discussin on the Tarot.
It was quiet at this time of day, the firelight from the
community room flickering down the hallways to the study
rooms and eating areas. We shivered as we made our way down
the hall, then entered into the study where a small heater
stood as a lonely outpost in the center of the room. We
talked and huddled near it, as though it were a small glowing
bed of coals.

"Rhuddlwm, the Tarot symbols were derived from heiro-
glyphics displayed on the walls of the passageway leading
from the Sphinx to the Great Pyramid. It was in this underground tunnel that the secret schools of Egypt initiated and
instructed their seekers into arcane wisdom of the ancients.
This 'Great White Brotherhood' retained much of the inner
teachings from Atlantis. These heiroglyphic symbols portray
phases of self-growth which raises the individual's level of
consciousness.

We began moving from painting to painting.

"These are the Twenty-two Arcana.

171

"Arcanum I, the Magus, expresses the divine world, the absolute being who contains, and from whom flows the concept of all possible things. In the intellectual world he represents unity, the synthesis of numbers, the will. In the physical world, he stands for humanity called upon to raise itself by an expansion of its capabilities into the three circles of the absolute.

"This is represented by the perfect person, upright in the attitude of will proceeding to action. He wears a white robe, symbol of purity. His belt is a serpent biting its tail, symbolic of eternity. He holds in his right hand a golden scepter, image of command, raised towards the heavens in gesture of aspiration toward knowledge, love, and power. The index finger of his left hand points toward the ground, signifying reign over the material world and meaning the human will should be an earthy reflection of divine will, promoting good, preventing evil.

"Arcanum II, the Door of the Occult Sanctuary, expresses the consciousness of the absolute being who embraces the three periods of all being—the past, the present, and the future. In the intellectual world, this represents the reflection of unity, which is a duality, the perception of visible and invisible dimensions. In the physical world, this symbol represents woman, the matrix of man, who joins herself with him in a similar destiny.

"This is represented by a woman seated on the threshold of the temple of Isis between two columns. The column on her right is red, signifying purity of spirit. The column on her left is black, and represents the night of chaos, the impure spirits encased in the bonds of material things. The woman is crowned with a tiara with a crescent moon surrounding it, covered by a veil whose folds fall over her face. She wears on her breast the solar cross and carries on her knees an open book which she half covers with her cloak. It is

172

symbolic of the truth which hides itself from the sight of the curious. This is occult knowledge."

"How much occult knowledge is there?" I asked.

"As much as there are grains of sand on the earth," Sarah replied. "But there is a beautiful imagery and logic which reveals it all together and let's it make sense. Do you want to hear more now?"

"Yes, go on."

"Arcanum III is Isis-Urania. This is the arcanum of action expressed in the divine world--the supreme power balanced by the eternally active mind and by absolute wisdom. In the intellectual world it is the universal fecundity of the Supreme Being; in the physical world it means Nature is labor, the germination of the acts that are to spring from the will.

"This arcanum is represented by a woman seated at the center of a blazing sun, crowned by twelve stars. Notice how her feet rest on the Moon. She is the symbol of inward fertility. The Sun is symbolic of creative strength. The crown, or stars, symbolizes the twelve Houses of the Zodiac."

"There is so much detail, so many symbols here. How are able to interpret it all?"

"It takes time, Rhuddlwm. You'll learn it so that it becomes second nature to you. As you read the tarot cards, for example, the symbols will weave together a meaning meant only for that reading.

"Look at the next one. Arcanum IV, the Cubic Stone, expresses a realization of the divine venture contained in the absolute being--affirmation, negation, discussion, solution. In the physical world, it represents the realization of the actions directed by the knowledge of truth, the love of justice, the strength of the will, and the work of the organs.

"It is represented by a man wearing a helmet surmounted by a crown. He is seated on a cubic stone. His right hand

173

holds a wand and his right leg is bent and rests on the other
in the form of a cross. This is symbolic of accomplishment
of human labors.

"Arcanum V, an Occult Inspiration, is the Master. This
arcanum expresses the universal law in the intellectual world
and in religion. In the physical world it expresses inspiration.

"This is the hierophant, the Prince of Occult Doctrine,
who is seated between two columns of the Sanctuary. He is
leaning on a cross with three horizontals and depicts with
the index finger of his right hand the sign of silence on
his breast. At his feet, two men have prostrated themselves,
one clothed in red, the other in black.

"The hierophant represents the genius of good intention
and the spirit of consciousness. His gesture is an invita-
tion to meditation, to listen to the voice within. The
columns on his right symbolize the divine law, the one on the
left signifies freedom to obey or disobey. The triple cross
is the emblem of the universal consciousness providing the
three worlds in order to produce in them all of manifestation
of life. The two men, one red and one black, represent the
genii of light and of darkness, both of whom obey the master
of the arcana."

Although the individual aspects and emblems of these
figures wre fascinating, I couldn't take in all the great
numbers of symbols; however, the overall effect stunned me.
It was rather majestic.

"Here, Arcanum VI, also called the Two Roads, expresses
the Ordeal. This arcanum in the divine world expresses the
knowledge of good and evil, while in the intellectual world
represents the balance of necessity and liberty. In the
phyical world the scene stands for the antagonism of the
natural forces, the chain of cause and effect. It is represented by a man standing motionless at a crossroads. His
eyes are fixed upon the earth, his arms crossed on his breast.

"Two women, one on his right, one on his left, stand
with a hand on his shoulder, pointing out to him one of the
two roads. The woman on his right has a circlet of gold
around her forehead. She personifies venture. The one on
the left is crowned with vine leaves and represents indulgence.
Above and behind this group, the genius of justice, borne on
a point of blazing light, is drawing his bow and directs the
arrow of punishment and indulgence. The whole scene expresses
the struggle between the passions and the conscience."

I saw this and shuddered. How many arrows will I spend
a lifetime plucking out?

"Watch out for simplicity. We aren't looking at just
one image or symbol, but a whole complex and how they interact."

My shoulders, caught in the act of tension, relaxed
somewhat as I perceived through Sarah's smile an open perception of these symbols.

"Arcanum VII, the Chariot of Victory, expresses in the
divine world the Septenary, the domination of spirit over
nature. In the intellectual world, this is the priesthood.
In the physical world, this is the submission of the elements
and the forces of matter to the intelligence and to the
labors of man. The chariot is surmounted by a canopy upheld
by four columns. In this chariot, an armed warrior carries a
wand and a sword in his hands. He is crowned with a crown of
gold ornaments, with five points, topped by three pentagrams.
The square chariot symbolizes the work accomplished by the
will which has overcome all obstacles. The four columns supporting the canopy represent the four elements conquered by
the master of the wands and the sword. On the front of the
chariot is drawn a sphere upheld by two outstretched wings,
sign of the limitless exhaltation of human power in the
infinity of space and time."

"What do all the decorative elements on the warrior
represent?"

175

The skepticism I generally walked around with was aroused again as Sarah detailed the richly painted symbols, but then I reminded myself how mythology and symbolism operated in complex subconscious interactions in dreams. It was partly a case of discovering fast undercurrents of the mind's other world where the spirit dominated, bringing intellect into new operations.

"The crown of gold on the warrior's head," Sarah continued, "signifies the possession of intellectual illumination which gives light to all the arcana of chance. The three stars which decorate the five points symbolize power balanced by mind and wisdom. Three squares are engraved on the breastplate. They signify rectitude, judgment, will, and action which give the power of which the breastplate is the emblem.

"The lifted sword is the sign of victory. The scepter-- crowned by a triangle, symbol of the spirit; by a square, symbol of matter; and by a circle, symbol of eternity-- signifies the perpetual domination of the mind over the forces of nature. Two sphinxes, one white, the other black, are harnessed to the chariot. The former represents gold--the latter, evil.

"Arcanum VIII, Themis, the arcanum of equilibrium, expresses in the divine world absolute justice. In the intellectual world, attraction and repulsion are expressed; in the physical world, the dualities expressed are the elative and the fallible, the narrowness of human justice. Thus, Themis is shown as a woman seated on a throne wearing a crown and armed with spear points. She holds an upward pointing sword in her right hand and a pair of scales in her left. This is the ancient symbol of jutice, weighing the deeds of humanity with the scales and opposing evil with the sword as a counterweight.

"The sword is a sign of justice which proceeds from the Goddess in the stabilizing reaction which restores order-- a sign of protection for the righteous, and a warning for

176

evil ones. The eyes of justice are blindfolded to show that she weighs and punishes without noticing the conventional differences established by humankind.

"Arcanum IX, the Veiled Lamp, the arcanum of prudence, is expressed in the divine world as absolute wisdom, in the intellectual world as prudence, and in the physical world as circumspection. It is represented by an old man who walks leaning on a stick and holding in front of him a lighted lantern half hidden by his cloak. This old man personifies experience acquired in the labors of life. The lantern symbolizes enlightenment which illuminates the past, present, and future. The cloak that half conceals it, signifies discretion. The stick symbolies prudence which supports the man who does not reveal his purpose."

The next painting contained an intriguing set of mysteries.

"What's this all about?" I asked Sarah, wondering how long the tarot symbols had flourished before going underground.

"That is Arcanum X, the Sphinx, the arcanum of Fortune, expressed in the divine world by the action principle that animates all beings. In the intellectual world it is expressed by the principles of ruling authority. In the phyical world it stands for good or evil fortune, represented by a wheel suspended between two columns by its axis. On the right, Humanubis, the spirit of God, strives to climb to the top of the wheel. On the left, Typhon, the spirit of evil is cast down. The sphinx holds the sword in its paw and is balanced on the top of the wheel. This is destiny ready to strike to the right or left. No one is immune.

"Arcanum XI, the Tamed Lion, is expressed in the divine world by the principle of all strength--spiritual or physical. In the intellectual world this becomes mind force. In the physical world it is organic force, represented by the image of a young girl who with her bare hands is closing the jaws of a lion. Faith in oneself is the major key."

177

I thought for a moment. "These are strong images. This next one is one I'd like to avoid in real life."

"True, but even the most powerfully negative images have interesting consequences at times depending upon the interaction of each symbol." Sarah looked with perspective at the next one.

"Arcanum XII, the Sacrifice, the arcanum of violent death, is expressed in the divine world by the revolution of the law, in the intellectual world by the teaching of duty, and in the physical world is sacrifice. It is represented by a man hung by one foot from a gallows which rests on two trees, each of which has six branches cut from the trunk. The hands are tied behind him and the bend of his arms forms the base of an inverted triangle, the summit of which is his head. It is the sign of violent death encountered by tragic accident and accepted in a spirit of heroic devotion to truth and justice. The twelve branches represent the destruction of the twelve houses of the horoscope. The inverted triangle symbolizes catastrophe."

I noted the emphasis on mathematics, as well as on human images, for these symbols.

We moved down along the wall and stopped to gaze at the scyth.

"This is Arcanum XIII, the Scyth, the arcanum of trans-formation. In the divine world it becomes the perpetual movement of creation, destruction, and renewal. In the intellectual world this is the ascent of the spirit into the death of the human nature, represented by a skeleton reaping heads in a meadow. This is the symbol of destruction and rebirth of all forms of being in the domain of time."

We moved around the room now, returning to the wood burning stove to warm our hands.

Sarah continued. "Some of these signs are paradoxes, having quite different interpretations for the different worlds. This is one reason why there is such a complexity of interactions.

"This one is Arcanum XIV, the Solar Spirit, the arcanum of initiative. It is expressed in the divine world by the perpetual movement of life, in the intellectual world by the combination of the ideas that create morality, and in the physical world by the combinatin of the forces of Nature. It is represented by the spirit of the Sun holding two urns and pouring from one into the other, the vital elixir of life."

On the north wall, we discussed the more unaccountable forces prevailing in Arcanum XX.

"Typhon is the arcanum of fate. In it, the divine world is expressed by predestination, the intellectual world by mystery, and in the physical world by the unforeseen or fatality, represented by Typhon, the spirit of catastrophe, who rises out of a flaming abyss and brandishes a torch over the heads of two men chained at his feet. This is the symbol of fatality which burst into certain lives like the eruption of a volcano, and overwhelms the great and small alike.

"Arcanum XVI, is represented by a Lightening Struck Tower, the arcanum of ruin. It is expressed in the divine world by the punishment of pride, in the intellecual world is the downfall of the spirit that attempts to discover the mystery of God, and in the physical world is reversal of fortune, represented by a tower struck by lightening. A crowned and uncrowned man are thrown down from its heights with the ruins of the battlement. It is the symbol of material forces that can crush great and small alike, as well as frustrating hopes and plans. Again, we see how in each world there is a different interpretation."

We wandered around receiving the images, my silence and retrospection resembling times on other plateaus of learning. I tried to search my mind for an experience which had occurred years before and which would link my memory to these ancient

179

symbols. But I was cold, and the fire in the study was
dying.

We returned to the main room and gathered with the
others for worship. Later we would return to seek out the
rest of these elaborate symbols.

* * * * *

One day, fresh from a study session, I asked Sarah to
continue explaining the haunting images in the study. They
seemed to have some clues I had searched for.

"Arcanum XVII," she began, "is the Star of the Magi,
the arcanum of hope. It is expressed in the divine world
by immorality, in the intellectual world as the inner light
that illuminates the spirit, and in the physical world as
hope, represented by a blazing star with light rays surrounded
by seven other stars hovering over a naked girl who pours over
two goblets, one golden, the other silver. Beside her,
a butterfly is alighting on a rose. This girl is the symbol
of hope which scatters its dew upon our saddest days. She is
naked, in order to signify that hope remains with us when we
have been berefit of everything.

"Arcanum XVIII, Twilight, the arcanum of deception, is
expressed in the divine world by the abyss of the infinite,
and in the intellectual world by the darkness that surrounds
the spirit when it submits itself to the power of the instincts. In the physical world it is represented by deception and hidden enemies, represented by a meadow illuminated
by a half-clouded moon in a vague twilight. A tower stands
on each side of a path disappearing into a barren landscape.
In front of one tower, a dog bays at the moon. In front of
the other, a dog crouches. Between them is a crab. These
towers symbolize the fake security which hides hidden perils."

I was drawn very strongly to the next painting.

"Arcanum XIX, the Blazing Light, the arcanum of earthly
 happiness is expressed in the divine world by the supreme
heaven. In the intellectual world it is seen as sacred truth,
and in the physical world by peaceful happiness, represented

180

by a radiant Sun shining down on two children, innocence
personified. They hold each other's hand, surrounded by a
circle of flowers. This is the symbol of happiness promised
by the simple life."

Arcanum XX was in a darker corner of the room and seemed
to flare out at me even before I noticed the details of its
fine oil strokes. Coming closer, I asked Sarah whether
this one had any special effects on her also.

"Perhaps this arcanum affects you now because of your
dramatic awakening. Or maybe it indicates a new surge of
learning about to come," she suggested.

"It is the Awakening of the Deep, or the arcanum of
renewal. It represents the passage from life on earth to
the life of the future. A spirit blows a trumpet over a
half-opened tomb. A man, a woman, and a child, a collection
of the human trinity, are shown rising from this tomb. It is
a sign of the change which is the end of all things of good
as well as of evil."

Two paintings were left, mounted on a final wall area,
and we stopped before them, scrutinizing the smallest details
for the last of the beautiful illustrations of the Ancient
Secrets. It was like viewing the majestic possessions and
art of an ancient tomb, seeing the spirit of humanity on
its journey through death to life again, the finely embedded
designs symbolizing the immortal soul in all its aspects.

Sarah explained these last two to me.

"Arcanum XXI, the Crown of the Magi, is the arcanum of
reward, and is represented by a garland of golded roses surrounding a star. It is placed in a circle around which are
set at equal distances the heads of a man, a bull, a lion,
and an eagle. This is the sign with which the magus decorates
himself and has reached the highest degree of initiation, thus
acquiring a power limited only by intelligence and wisdom."

The next was a beautiful image in contrast to the last
and I felt somewhat cheated that the last was such an ominous

181

sign. Perhaps with all the symbols whirling around me, it
was a slight warning to be alert and aware, avoiding a habit
of glossing over the truth.

"Arcanum XXII, the Crocodile, is the arcanum of expiation, represented by punishment which follows every error.
This is a blind man carrying a full beggar's wallet and who
is about to step over a cliff into the jaws of a waiting
crocodile. The blind man is the symbol of the slave of
material things. His wallet is packed with his errors and
his faults. The cliff represents the ruin of his works. The
crocodile is the emblem of fate and the inevitable expiation."

Sarah began to summarize the knowledge, shifting her
words and body somewhat to catch the dappled light coming
through the window. Her voice and manner, trained to articu-
late with soft wisdom and sharp insight, captured a half year
of learning with the skill of the mountain climber on the
steep rocky face of a cliff.

"These are the major arcana, their meaning is derived
by the use of the Sacred Keys. Taken together, and in sequence,
their meaning is that human will, illuminated by arcane knowledge and manifested in action, creates within the seeker a
realization of the Power which can be used for good or evil,
in the circle bounded by the laws of universal order. After
having overcome the ordeal, imposed on it by divine wisdom,
will enters after victory into possession of a work it has
created, and retaining its equilibrium on the axis of prudence,
it dominates the fluctuations of fortune. Humankind's strength,
sanctified by sacrifice which is the voluntary offering of itself on the altar of dedication and expiation, triumphs over
death.

"Human will's divine transformation, which raises itself
above the tomb into the tranquil region of an infinite progress, opposes the reality of an immortal initiative to the

182

eternal falsehood of totality. The course of time is
measured by its ruins, but beyond each ruin we see the
reappearance of the dawn of hope on the twilight of disappoint-
ment. Humanity aspires relentlessly to whatever is beyond
itself, and the sun of happiness rises only behind the tomb,
after the renewal of its being by the death that opens a
higher cirle of will, intelligence, and action. All will that
lets itself be governed by bodily instincts is an abdication
of liberty and condemns itself to the expiation of its
errors or its mistakes. On the other hand, all will that
unifies itself with the Great Spirit in order to demonstrate
truth and justice, enters after this life into the eternal
realm of enfranchised spirits.

"So, Rhuddlwm, are there truly any secrets? Humanity
has existed for millions of years and civilizations have
risen to dizzy heights only to fall into ruin; knowledge has
been gained only to be lost; books disagree in almost every
subject of human science and art; there is controversy over
the existence of UFO's; ESP is a common topic of discussion;
psychic readers have increased in number faster than fast
food chains; new religions and Gurus are a common-place fact
of life.

"So you see, Humankind has created its own modern day
labyrinth or maze of confusion, and efficiently hidden the
ancient arcane knowledge from the eyes of the ordinary person."

"Everywhere the seeker turns there is someone ex-
pounding 'The Ultimate Truth' of eternity. So where can the
new seeker turn?" I asked.

"Y Tylwyth Teg is only one pathway to the God/dess.
There are many," she answered. "But, only by choosing a
single pathway initially may one attempt to understand the
secret keys."

"Sarah, could you teach me some more about the different
elements making up Y Tylwyth Teg?"

183

"The pathway of Y Tylwyth Teg is composed of many elements," she began. "Foremost among these are the twelve great virtues. These twelve great virtues are part of the universal laws. By acquiring these virtues, you build character, integrity, and ethics, which results in a concentration of psychic power. This creates a direct channel to the Force of the universe, the Great Spirit. This Force permeates the universe and is the cause and result of all life.

"The first virtue is tolerance, a form of wisdom which allows you to refrain from passing judgment on your fellow humans.

"Charity is the second virtue and stresses love, clemency, leniency, and an interest in the welfare of others. One gives of oneself and does not criticize others.

"Humility, the third virtue, is an awareness of one's own shortcomings, and does not imply weakness. It is the result of strength and is the absence of arrogance, pride, and self interest.

"Devotion is the dedication of oneself to an ideal or a cause such as to the service of the Great Spirit.

"Patience, the fifth virtue, is calmness and composure under suffering or provocation while performing a demanding task.

"Kindliness, the sixth virtue, is a sincere desire to never intentionally bring hurt to another person. It is the consideration of others feelings and demonstrates gentleness and sympathy.

"Forbearance, the seventh virtue, is serenity of mind under provocation and demonstrative self-possession. It is non-resistance and teaches binding with any situation. It is an exercise in humility.

"Sincerity, the eighth virtue, is the absence of deceit, hypocrisy, and shame. This manifests in the genuine person and shows a desire to learn and practice what is right.

184

"Courage, the ninth virtue, is deliberate moral determination of danger and is the product of reason. It is distinctive from bravery because bravery is usually an instinctive response to a perilous situation.

"Precision, the tenth virtue, is exactness, accuracy, and definiteness. It opposes careless work and hazy thinking.

"Efficiency, the eleventh virtue, is the ability to deal with the environment with a minimum expenditure of time, energy, and materials.

"Discrimination is the last virtue and is the power to discern the motives of people, see their character, and is also the ability to see the real truth beneath the apparent surface of situations.

"These virtues are the result of right thinking."

"But how do we learn to think 'right'?" I asked.

"You must start again," she replied.

"What does that mean?"

"You must become a trusting, open being. You must learn that consciousness is energy, love, awareness, light, wisdom, truth, purity, and the twelve virtues. You must learn that you are without form, without limit--beyond time, beyond space. You are everything and everything is you. You are the God and the Goddess!"

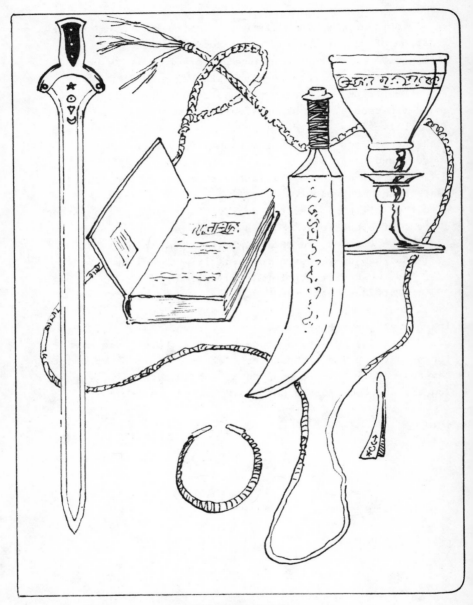

CHAPTER 13
Sacred Tools

CHAPTER THIRTEEN

THE THIRTEEN ANCIENT TREASURES OF Y TYLWYTH TEG

"The candle is not there to illuminate itself."
                              --Nawab Jan Fisher Khan

"Oh thrice born, this is the legend of the thirteen
treasures of the Cymmry:

"In the beginning there were the wide stretches of the
sky--nay, nothing existed but was a thought in the spirit of
the Lord and Lady.

"The earth, being a thought in the mind of the Great
Spirit, came into existence. And, although the Great Spirit
was in a different world and a different universe, the spirit
of it passed to this one and dwelled here for a time. But
time, the enemy of all intruders, passed and the doorway
between worlds was lost for a time. So, the Spirit dwelled
in this universe and called itself Watchers and angels and
spirits and elementals, but it passed the time as an instrument
of the universal spirit by dwelling in animals and humans.

"The Spirit became too attached to this world and desired
emotions and beauty and love and power and knowledge. But,
when it made itself known to some humans they called it 'God'
and knelt down in adoration, so the Spirit sought to teach
humankind of the nature of itself, so that humankind could
help in solving the supreme mystery of the separation.

"And the Spirit helped humankind to create kingdoms
and cities and wonderous works, but because the balance of
creation and destruction works throughout the universe, each
time mankind learned of the nature of its creator and gained
the power of love and knowledge, destruction came to change
the face of the land and waters.

"So, the Spirit of all gave humankind thirteen tablets
with all the knowledge of the universe written upon them.

187

And, so they would not be destroyed, the Spirit placed these
tablets in the mind of humankind and in three sacred temples
which would be opened whenever humankind lost the knowledge
implanted within. And, so that humankind would be reminded,
the Spirit gave humankind the thirteen moons of the year.
It gave humankind the twelve constellations of the Zodiac
so that humankind would know that the circle of twelve added
to the one yields thirteen--for one is the center of all."

The Elder looked around at all of us as she spoke:

"Now, my children, you are in possession of the thirteen
books of the Cymmry. These are the sacred tablets of knowledge and each one represents a part of the whole."

We looked through the books as the Elder continued.

"The first, Modrwy Eluned, The Ring of Luned, is represented by the tools: the wand, the ring, and the lamp--and
by the elemental of fire. In the Zodiac it is represented
by Aries.

"This is the Book of Y Tuatha De Danann, the People of
the Goddess Danu, and contains the story of the Tuatha and
the sacred triads.

"This book is represented also by the planetary stones--
ruby, hematite, jasper, and bloodstone. It is repressed by
the planet Mars.

"Pais Padarn, the Cloak of Padarn Beisrudd, is the
Book of Gwydion, son of Don, and contains the sacred poems
of Gwydion. It is represented by the zodiacal sign of Taurus,
the element Earth, and the planet Venus. The tool is the
sacred oil and the planetary stones are emerald and sapphire.

"Mwys Gwyddno III, the Hamper of Gwyddno, is the Book of
Plenydd and contains the sacred symbol, the Celtic Tree, the
sacred tools, and the philosophy of Magick. It is represented by the element air, the zodiacal sign of Gemini, the
planetary stones--agate, cornelian, sardonyx, and chalcedony--
the planet Mercury, and the tools--the thurible, the incense,
and the bell.

"Corn Brangaled IV, or the Horn of Brangaled, contains the precepts, the altar symbology, and the legends of the Hidden People. It is represented by the element water, the zodiacal sign Cancer, the planetary stones of opal, diamond, mother-of-pearl, and beryl. The planet is the Moon.

"Llen Arthur V, or the Veil of Arthur, is the Book of Dawn containing the triads of Arthur. It is represented by the element fire, the zodiacal sign of Leo, the planet the Sun, and the planetary stones--chrysolite, hyacinth, and topaz. It is also represented by the tools--the scourge and the robe of the Priest.

"Dysgyl Rhegnydd Ysgolhaig VI, or the Dish of Rhegnydd Ystolhaig, is the Book of Rites and Rituals and contains the Full Moon rituals, the festivals and the feasts of the Cymmry. It is represented by the element Earth, the zodiacal sign Virgo, and the planet Mercury. The planetary stones are agate, cornelian, sardonyx, and chalcedony. The tools are the pentacle and the talisman.

"Cyllell Llawfrodedd Farchawg VII, the Knife of Llaw-frodedd Farchawg, is the Book of Speel and contains all knowledge of magick and spells. The element is air, the zodiacal sign is Libra and the planet is Venus. The planetary stones are emerald and sapphire, and the tool is the athame.

"Pair Cerridwen VIII, or the Cauldron of Cerridwen, is the Book of Arawn and contains all the sciences of divining, the dragon paths, and states. The element is water, the zodiacal sign is Scorpio and the planet is Pluto. The planetary stones are ruby, hematite, jasper, and bloodstone. The tools are the circle and the cauldron.

"Cadair Morgan Mwylawr, the Chair of Morgan Mwylawr, is the Book of Gwron and contains the philsophy of the grove, color symbology, the watchtowers, the blue pentagram and the elements. It is represented by the element fire, the zodiacal sign Sagittarius, the planet Jupiter and the tools,

189

the staff and the broom. The planetary stones are amethyst, blue diamond, and turquoise.

"Gren Rhegnydd Ysgolhaig, the Platter of Rhegnydd Ysgolhaig, is the Book of Migration. It is represented by the element earth, the zodiacal sign Capricorn, the planet Saturn and the planetary stones--onyx, jet, diamond, obsidian, and black coral. The tool is the platter.

"Dyrnwyn, the Sword of Rhydderch Hael, is the Book of Y Tylwyth Teg. It contains the seven paths, the seed of life, the four sister clans, the Song of November, the dance of grain, the cycle of orbe, the festival of Lugh, and the Battle of the Trees. The element is air, the zodiacal sign is Aquarius, and the planet is Uranus. The planetary stones are amethyst, sapphire, opal, and amber. The tool is the sword.

"Mantle Tegan Eurvron XII, Mantle of Tegan Eurvron, is the Book of the Radiant Brow. It contains the poems of Taliesin. It is represented by the element water, the zodiacal sign Pisces, the planet Jupiter, and the planetary stones of amethyst and blue diamond. The tools are the robe of the Priestess and the cords.

"Maen Llog XIII, Stone of the Wise, is the Whetstone of Tudwall Tudclud. This is the Spirit. It is the Book of Hajarel Fehm and contains the path to enlightenment. It is represented by the element earth, the center, and the tools-- the altar, the temple, and the grove.

"The Owl describes the Chessboard of Gwendolyn. This is the workbook--the synthesis of the thirteen treasures-- the twelve signs of the Zodiac added to the Spirit."

* * * * *

It was a chilly February evening as we faced each other in the airport terminal. There were tears in her eyes and I was unashamedly crying. We were saying goodbye for what could well be the last time. I was returning to my country and she was remaining in hers.

190

I had changed! Oh, how I had changed! Nine months ago if someone had told me I would be crying in public, I would have laughed in scorn. "Men don't do things like that!"

She had taught me well. This woman who was my guide and my lover.

"Rhuddlwm, I knew this day would come, but it's still hard to tell you that you must go away from me, if you are to attain your destiny."

"Sarah, it's harder for me, because you've taught me so much. You've shown me the pathway that I've searched for all my life and you've shown me a truth which is fantastically simple but much deeper than any worldly truth. When I first met you, I didn't know where I was going or where I had been. You became a guiding light in the world of confused darkness."

"Rhuddlwm, you are destined to be much more of a guide than I could ever be. But, beware of that male chauvanist pride of yours that displays itself from time to time. Your male sexuality is very strong and will be a problem in years to come."

"I love you, Sarah, as a person and as a friend. I'll try to be worthy of your confidence."

"And I love you, Rhuddlwm."

Later, after we took off, as I stared out of the window, I imagined I could still see her standing alone, one hand raised in farewell.

I was experiencing two conflicting emotions--sorrow in leaving a loved one, and elation, for I had been adopted into the clan of Y Tylwyth Teg!

The last year had been an astounding experience. From the summit of Mount Puig Major on Majorca I had followed a pathway which had led me to the sacred Grail of Immortality. William, the immature boy died on that journey. But Rhuddlwm Gawr, the seeker, was born and continues to follow 'the Way.'

191

"Camelot"

192

EPILOG

Somewhere in North Georgia there is a living community of people dedicated to survival and peace. New seekers have arrived to join.

Rhuddlwm is speaking to them:

"Today we are seeing modern civilization forcing an ecological disaster upon a world unrestrained by the balance wheel of the true religion of the ancients.

"Past wars have been horrible beyond belief. Man's inhumanity to man is forever recorded in everyday life—survival of the fittest, money, power, lust, and revenge.

"All present religions are becoming decadent and un-certain. People are leaving their faiths in ever increasing numbers because they say this or that religion is not relevant any more, or the Bible has so many inconsistencies and mis-takes, or the church has hypocrites for members.

"Religion today is becoming a misused word. Every day new pop religions and cults arise which last for a time until their members see them for what they are and discard them for something else.

"Humankind is seeking as never before. We of Y Tylwyth Teg do not bring you a new religion. Rather, we bring you the Old Religion for the New Age.

"Ever remember, seekers, all religions are but aspects of the one ancient religion, the religion of truth—of love—and of balance. But, unfortunately, most religions of today are but shadows of the true reality of the ancients. They worship misconceptions because the true attributes have been lost.

"The Great Spirit has at intervals caused certain prophets and master teachers to be incarnated upon the earth in order to pass on the knowledge of truth to the souls.

193

"Jesus, Buddha, Confucius, and many others have come
and expounded the concepts of love and justice and peace to
humanity, but to what avail, for in their names numerous
religions have been formed which have perverted these same
concepts.

"In the Middle Ages Christians and Moslems fought bloody
battles, raped, pillaged, and destroyed, all in the name of
'God.' Today Catholics battle Protestants in Ireland and
Moslems kill Jews in the Middle East, all in the name of 'God.'

"When the worship of 'God' is not balanced by the worship
of 'Goddess,' tremendous karmic forces are unleased, and we
are experiencing just such an imbalance today. This reaction
will soon cause economic, geologic, and social upheavals which
will change your world as you know it today.

"The New Day is coming--the Age of Aquarius--an age
of knowledge and power. As this New Age approaches, we the
Family of Y Tylwyth Teg, are preparing for the time of devastation and tribulation which will usher in the New Age.

"We are organizing survival communities in the United
States and various other countries where the Old Religion
will survive and help prepare for the new age of peace and
love.

"You may ask in the beginning: 'Just what is the Family
of Y Tylwyth Teg?'

"The standard definition could be: 'An Ancient Celtic
system of religion and philosophy veiled in allegory, and
illustrated by symbols.'

"Our overall purpose is:

--To seek that which is of the most worth in the world;

--To exalt the dignity of every person, the human side of
   our daily activities, and the maximum service to
   humanity;

--To aid humanity's search in the Great Spirit's Universe
   for identity, for development, and for happiness;

194

--To RELINK Humanity with itself and Nature; and thereby
achieve better people in a better world, happier people
in a happier world, and wiser people in a wiser world.

"Our ultimate goal, simply stated, is Humankind's
spiritual and intellectual development.

"Historically, the Church of Y Tylwyth Teg as we know
it, evolved over 450 years ago, when the Thirteen Sacred
Manuscripts were first translated from Celtic Ogham Runes
and Ancient Oral Traditions into the Welsh written language.
Later, an English translation became the creative and deriva-
tive basis for our religion and Church.

"The American branch was organized in Washington, D.C.
in 1967, as 'The Gentle People,' and in Smyrna, Georgia in
1973 as the Church of Y Tylwyth Teg.

"But the actual roots of the Church go far deeper.
Tracing them is a romantic and exciting quest for adventure
in the realm of the mind and the spirit. It is a superb story
of enlightenment--more intriguing than the storied search
for the Holy Grail and more rewarding than a successful
discovery of the Philosophers Stone.

"Our teachings and symbols preceded our formal organization by thousands of years. They go deep into Ancient Ages.
The signs, symbols, and inscriptions come to us from across
long drifting centuries and can be found on ancient Sumarian
clay tablets in the cities of Ur; in the sunken cities of
Atlantis and in the first faltering steps of humankind millions
of years ago.

"The Church rituals and esoterism, therefore, are
treasure houses in which are stored the ageless essence of
Nature's immutable laws and the accumulation of thousands of
years of seeking experience.

"We learn our tenets in a system thus derived by pro-
gressive levels of instruction and we teach our members the
wise expositions of this philosophy and religion.

"Our levels represent the study and reflection of many
humans during many years and at heavy cost, and more labor

195

than the accumulated endeavors of many lifetimes in efforts
to attain worldy success. Our members, therefore, receive
a gift of the greatest value. They gain a comprehensive knowledge of our heritage, of history, philosophy, religion,
freedom, and Nature, and of their relationship to the Great
Spirit, the God and Goddess, and themselves.

"These will also lead to that understanding of identity,
clarity of mind and energy of will that propel toward personal enlightenment.

"We carry out our mission in a series of spiritual,
mystical, and enlightening programs.

"Ours, therefore, is a strong voice for human dignity,
justice, ethical values, and personal responsibilities.
Through our teachings many women and men have discovered an
opportunity to lead more rewarding lives. The example of
our actions has been as stirring and inspiring as that of
our Collective Commitment to true Human Progress.

"In our religious order, Nature is our God/dess. We
see our God/dess in all things. We believe that nature and
spirit are linked; that without that connection there is disharmony and unbalance.

"We teach the following:
--You can see the God/dess in meditation and during
    rituals but you meet Her/Him on the inner planes
    rather than on the physical level;
--Reincarnation of the Soul and Spirit is a universal
    principle;
--Karmic balance is the goal of all who live in the
    light of the God/dess;
--Magick, which is action in accordance with will and
    actualization of mental energy, can be used to heal
    and help;
--Religious and therapeutic counseling should be given
    to all who request it;

196

--Our every day life should be a reflection of our
   Spiritual inner awareness;
--Our Deities are represented by the female principle
   of fertility and creation and the male principle of
   procreation;
--Perfect love and perfect trust must be the philosophy
   of all Humankind;
--The human body is a beautiful work of nature; therefore, our rituals and festivals are conducted in a
   natural state showing our respect for and identity
   with the Earth Mother;
--If we walk in balance with nature, all our needs will
   be provided for;
--The Law of the Threefold Utterance and the Threefold
   Return is a main principle of Life;
--And that within the framework of nature, there are
   devic and elemental realms which may be used for
   healing, fertility, happiness, and protection.

"We are of the Old Religion and rediscovering the ancient
knowledge. We are RELINKING ourselves with others and with
Nature. We are also developing an inner awareness of our
spiritual heritage which will transform our consciousness
into a new dimension of reality.

"Yes we, the children of the Earth, are also the Hidden
children of the morning star; we seek only to dance the Dance
of Joy, the Celebration of Life. We bring you light, laughter,
and love, and we bring you enlightenment.

"The way is open--Come join the Old Religion for the
New Age!"

* * * * *

The Church of Y Tylwyth Teg:

Has established a Bardic School for the purpose of
Religious Instruction for Children and Adults, and also
Providing courses of Religious Instruction to prepare members
for the Priesthood;

Has established a Temple of Worship in accordance with the traditions, rites, and practices of Y Tylwyth Teg;

The Church of Y Tylwyth Teg was established in the United States in 1967 by Rhuddlwm Gawr, a Bard of Dewiniaeth Cymmry, and was Incorporated as a Non-Profit Organization (Religious) by the State of Georgia on February Second (2nd) 1977.

To become a Gwiddon, you must fill out an application form which will be supplied, complete a course of religious instruction, be "Named," go on your "Quest," and be "Adopted" into the Clan of Y Tylwyth Teg. Once you have been "Adopted" you will be allowed to participate in all religious Rites, Festivals, and Gatherings appropriate to your level.

To obtain further information concerning the Welsh Tradition, write:

Rhuddlwm Gawr
Church of Y Tylwyth Teg
P. O. Box 4196
Athens, GA. 30062
U. S. A.

Appendix

APPENDIX A

WELSH TRIADS OF WISDOM

The three sages of the race of the Cymmry were:

Hu Gadarin, who first collected the race of Cymmry and dispersed them into tribes.

Dyfnwal Moelmud, who first regulated the laws, privileges, and institutions of country and nation.

Tydain tal Awen, who first introduced order and method into the memorials and preservations of the oral art, and its properties. And from that order, the privileges and methodical usages of the bards of the Isle of Prydain were first devised.

*   *   *   *   *

--The three primary Bards of the Cymmry:
   Plenydd, which means light or radiance
   Arawn, which means harmony
   Gwron, which means Energy or virtue
These were they who devised the privileges and usages which belong to the Bards.

--The three ultimate objectives of Bardien:
   To reform morale and customs
   To receive peace
   To praise all that is good and excellent

--The three joys of the Bards of Y Tylwyth Teg:
   The increase of Knowledge
   The Reformation of manners
   The triumph of peace over devastation

--There are three avoidant injunctions on a Bard:
   To avoid sloth as a seeker given to investigation
   To avoid contention as a seeker of discretion and
        reason
   To avoid insult as a seeker of irreproachable manners

--The Three Circles of the Cymmry:
   Cylch y Cevgant, Circle of the Infinite, which none
   but the Great Spirit can fill
   Cylch yr Abred, Circle of Courses, the Slab of Life
   on which is a mixture of good and evil and through
   which Humankind passes on being regenerated
   Cylch y Gwyrfyd, Circle of Blessedness, which the
   regenerate ultimately attains.

--The three regulations of the Great Spirit towards
giving existence to everything:
   To annihilate the power of evil
   To assist all that is good
   To make discernment manifest, that it may be known
   what should and what should not be

--There are three laughs of a fool:
   At the good
   At the bad, and
   At he knows not what

--There are three things odious in a seeker:
   Licentiousness
   Deceit
   Malice
These things will destroy the seeker.

--The three branches of Humankind's duty:
   To   strive for an assimilation of character to the
          God/dess
   To benefit fellow humans
   To improve knowledge

--The three Grand Characteristics of Goodness:
   To speak the truth at all times fearless of consequences
   To love every good
   To suffer with fortitude for the sake of truth and
   goodness

--The Voice of the Threefold Utterance:
   I - (Pleyndd) - Light - Feminine - Future - Spiritual
   (Divine Wisdom through knowledge, understanding,
   intelligence and truth.)
   A - (Gwron) - Energy - Masculine - Present - Active
   (Divine Love--the seat of the affections --goodness.)
   O - (Arawn) - Harmony - Harmony of both in operation
   (Divine power --Result of the union of the above.)

--The three   letters of the unutterable name of the
Great Spirit:
        I - a being or becoming appropriate -- the yew tree
        A - proceeding, going forth -- the fir tree
        O - a casting, yielding an emanation -- the Furze

202

THE WICCAN REDE

Here is the advise from the Wise Ones:

Bide the Wiccan Laws we must
In perfect Love and perfect Trust.
Live and let live,
Fairly take and fairly give.
Cast the Circle thrice about
To keep the evil spirits out.
To bind the spell every time
Let the spell be spake in Rhyme.
Soft of eye and Light of touch,
Speak little, listen much.
Deosil go by the waxing moon,
Chanting out the witches rune.
Widdershine go by the waning moon,
Chanting out the baneful rune.
When the Lady's moon is new,
Kiss the hand to her, times two.
When the moon rides at her peak,
Then your heart desire seek.
Heed the Northwinds mighty gale,
Lock the door and drop the sail.
When the wind comes from the South,
Love will kiss thee on the mouth.
When the wind blows from the West,
Departed souls will have no rest.
When the wind blows from the East,
Expect the new and set the feast.
Nine woods in the cauldron go,
Burn them fast and burn them slow.
Elder be your ladies tree,
Burn it nor or cursed you'll be.

When the wheel begins to turn,
Let the Beltane fires burn.
When the wheel has turned a yule,
Light the log and the Horned One rules.
Heed ye Flower, Bush, and Tree,
By the Lady, Blessed be.
Where the rippling waters go,
Cast a stone and truth you'll know.
When ye have a true need,
Hearken not to others greed.
With a fool no season spend,
Or be counted as his friend.
Merry meet and merry part,
Bright the cheeks and warm the heart.
Mind the Threefold Law you should,
Three times bad and three times good.
When misfortune is enow,
Wear the Blue star on the brow.
True in Love ever be,
Unless thy lover's false to thee.
Eight words the Wiccan Rede fulfill,
And ye harm none, do what ye will.

PLANETARY MAGICK (From the Book of Speel- Y Tylwyth Teg)

"*Look ye to the West and ye will see from whence we came, and before that, the cold land, and before that, we sailed for many passings of the Moon, and lived many days in places unfriendly to us, and have fought many battles.*"

"*Oh sons and daughters of the Old Ones, know this your heritage - for you are the descendants of the ancient priests and priestesses of the Island of Poseidon, which the Romans call Atlantis.*"

"*Ye must have in your minds that it was evil and hate between different people which destroyed our lands and that here in Prydain no such evil and hate may be allowed to prevail.*"

"*You are herein given these tools of the ancient wisdom, not for your own gratification, but for others. You may use this knowledge only to help and never to hurt.*"

"*Hereafter is contained the ancient spells and magic of our fathers, may you who come after respect it as you would any Art or Science.*"

"*Before any spell is cast or magick worked, you must build your will and faith till it should act as itself.*"

"*Build your Circle with love and faith in the Great Spirit, never with hate or ill will in your hearts.*"

"*Always ask the Four Watchers of the Gateways to Gwlad Yr Haf to protect your Circle. For it is only with their protection that your magick may work.*"

"*Call to (the Lord and Lady) when ye have need of help in your magick, for they are the God and Goddess of magick and enchantment.*"

"*To know (Knowledge) is to dare (Initiative) is to will (Will Power) is to keep silent (Secrecy). These are the words of our fathers and to master their meaning is to master the Art and Science of Magick.*

The common attributes of the seven days are:

DAY	PLANET	SIGN	NAME OF SPIRIT
Saturday	Saturn	♄	Ilde Baoth
Thursday	Jupiter	♃	Eloi
Tuesday	Mars	♂	Saba
Sunday	Sol	☉	Adonai
Friday	Venus	♀	Ovraios
Wednesday	Mercury	☿	Astaphoi
Monday	Moon	☽	Phul

1. The Tables of Planetary Hours must be committed to memory.

2. The preparation of the Magickal Circle and various tables of relationships and correspondences are learned, following the study of Astrology and its relationship to magick.

3. Various healing rituals, power rituals, and protection speels are studied.

4. Herb magick and Herbal medicine is mastered together with candle magick, and finally the power symbolism of planetary magick.

5. To make use of the Planetary Symbols: Inscribe the magickal square upon one side of a disc made of athe appropriate metal. On the other side inscribe the correct sigil, with its name. Consecrate it with perfumed incense, then, wearing a ring inlaid with the planetary stone, light a candle annointed with the purpose oil of the correct planetary colour and, depending upon the types of result desired, utter the Angelic name, followed by the Daemonic name. Conclude with an offering of dried twigs and leaves from the planetary trees and herbs to the God/dess on the Altar.

6. In magick, it is of utmost importance to use one's senses complexity, as well as the will and the mind. Concentration, relaxation, and visualization are necessary components of magickal practive. When one opens up to all that there is, it ceases to be a power game over something . . . rather it becomes a richer awareness of our own personal spiritual Godhead permeating all . . . Thru magick, we develop self-betterment, and self-discipline, with change as the key word, and spiritual development as the goal. Too many people get caught up in the performance of magick without realizing it is important to always live 'magickally' and more important to live in close communion with Nature, where we can examine and lovingly rejoice in worship of the Mother's Earth.

PLANETARY INFLUENCES

INFLUENCES OF SATURN

In the Roman culture, a name of the God is Saturn, and the Goddess is
known as Hecate. In early times Saturn had a great deal to do with the
Earth, hence the connotation of stability. The goddess Hecate is known
for her connection with spiritis and the calling forth of the dead. The
influences present here are the same as those present in the influences
of the planet Saturn. Of course, by envisioning the Goddess and God one
is greatly aided in any ritual one may do. The numer 3 is especially
sacred to the Goddess Hecate, and should be used in any spells requireing
her assistance. When doing any work with these influences it is best to
be armed with one's sword. This would include even work of a beneficial
nature that would be concerned with Saturnian or Hecatina things.

In all cultures the influence of the planet Saturn is shown by the
'gods and goddesses that rule the earth and the area under the earth. In
Greek mythology, Rhea represents the mother aspect of the earth, as she
was supposed to be the mother of the gods, although She came forth from
the Earth. Cybele represents the primitive, savage state of the earth
and was worshipped in a primal, savage manner. She ruled over all wild
beasts and the crucial aspects of life and death in their rawest form as
they appear in Nature. Gaea was another ancient Goddess of the Earth
whose meaning is basically one of the stability of the Earth and its
everlasting qualities. Demeter, the goddess of the fertilized earth,
and Goddess of marriage (in the sense of it being a life-lon- attachment)
was also identified with these Saturnian qualities. Later Demeter was
identified with Persephone, the goddess of the Underworld.

THE INFLUENCES OF JUIPTER

In Greek legends the forms of this power are represented by Posidon and
Zeus. Zeus is the father of the gods, the supreme ruler, and Posidon is
the ruler of the Oceans. These ideas keep with the influences of Jupiter
as being those of materialistic concern. They were brothers (at least
in Greek mythology), and we would suggest that you use Zeus if the work
is more in the nature of a mental success (though not quite falling into
the sphere of Mercury), and Posidon if the work is of an extremely materialistic nature.

The Roman name of the god ruling this sphere is Jupiter.

207

THE INFLUENCES OF MARS

In ancient times, Mars was the god of farming and agriculture. He lived
in the orchards and the tilled fields of the countryside. Later he was
worshipped as the god of war and battle, representing human strength.
His influences as a god are similar to those given here for the planetary
power-, and he is the best god-form to invoke them in. Although he was
many other names, they are quite savage and cruel--even the Greek form
of Mars, Ares, was considered to be a liar, a coward, and a bully--hardly
the sort of person you'd want to ask for help! As with all the gods and
goddesses you invoke, you should study the background and attributions
of the name/deity you choose. Please do not slight this study. A god-
form that seems perfect on the surface may have hidden twists in its
essence that will cause the unwitting a world of grief.

THE INFLUENCES OF THE SUN

Apollo is the god of light, of the sun (he also rules medicine, mental
illness, and archery, as well as stringed instruments). But Apollo is
not the sun itself. This is another god--Helios. As a sun god, Helios
is of course concerned with the crops and life on earth in general, as
all living things are kept alive by the light of the sun.

The qualities of the various gods in various cultures that represent
the sun are very similar. They all possess the powers we have listed
under the qualities of the Sun itself. But they also have additional
qualities as well, and make sure you know what they are. There is a vast
difference between Lugh the Long-Handed of the Cymmry, Apollo Longsight
of the Greeks, and Amaterasu, the Japanese sun-goddess; yet they
are all gods of the Sun. If you find that you are hiving difficulties of
any sort, then invoke the Sun as we have discussed in our previous lessons.
This will hold true for all the planetary powers. There is no reason
why you must search for a godform of the proper essence, only to have your
working stymied when you cannot find one. Go ahead with your work, calling
upon the power of the Planetary Spirit itself. In some instances, you may
ind this suits your working better.

THE INFLUENCES OF VENUS

Venus, called Aphrodite by the Greeks, ruled the sexuality of the Earth.
She is the Goddes of Love, true romantic Love. Use the Planetary
Venus, because this is the best way of invoking the Goddess Venus. As
with any Power, do your research, and don't forget about the negative
aspects of Venus. Love can easily turn to hatred, and the Esoteric

208

Venus was notoriously fickle. Venus is usually described as a beautiful
naked young woman, and I would suggest sticking to this description in
your visualizations. Do not limit yourself to seeing the gods and goddesses
as they look in statuary, but rather as they look to you. Don't limit
yourself by any material manifestation of these powers; let your imagination
be your only limitation. As they say, "The Gods work in mysterious ways."

THE INFLUENCES OF MERCURY

Mercury, or Hermes as the Greeks call him, is the messenger of the Gods
(and the patron of thieves). But more important than this title, he is
mental qualities idealized. In various cultures he is the Scribe (Thoth
in Egyptian mythology), the Teacher, and a Patron of Physicians (one
reason for the Caduceus, Hermes' symbol, being used as the symbol
of Physicians—as well as FTD florists.) But againm do not limit yourself,
and have in mind just what you want before you invoke. As Hermes Psycho-
pompos, Mercury is guardian and Guide of the Dead, and as Thoth-Hermes
he is the God of Magick, especially sorcery or necromancy. The specific
godnames you invoke under will probably be decided by personal preference,
as well as the traditions of the Coven you join.

THE INFLUENCES OFTHE MOON

The goddesses of the Moon, and their names, are many and various. Luna,
the goddess generally invoked under the New Moon, stands to Diana as
Helios stands to Apollo. Ceres can be called upon for works during a
Full Moon, and Hecate is the most often invoked Goddess of the Dark Moon.
There are many names the Moon Goddess can be called on, though. She
has influences over all the Zodiac signs. For example, the Moon in
Scorpio is represented by Lillity, while the moon in Virgo is represented
by Ceres, on through the Zodiac. Not only do the phases of the Moon and
the passage if it through the various houses of the Zodiac have their own
particular Goddess—form to call upon, but the seasons also have theirs.
The Moon Goddess is also represented by the Goddesses of the other Planetary
Powers. As the Mother Goddess, and the major deity in Wicca her titles
differ greatly and there is a phase of her manifestation for ever concept of
Deity known to man. Some are as obscure as Derketa, the African Moon-and-
Death Goddess, or as wellknown as Freyja of the Aesir (whom some treat as
a female counterpart of Pan, who corresponds to Telluric Mars).

209

The best suggestion we can make is to do your research; study the gods and Goddesses in every culture; then when you find in your reading that you are particularly drawn to one culture, you can study it in detail and even evoke its planetary powers.

There are many Goddesses who play an important role in Wicca. The best known of these is Diana, who in Etruria is worshipped as patroness of the Witches. She was never merely a Moon-Goddess, though scholars and woman-haters of the New Religion have tried to make us think so, and now that the Witch-Craft is coming into its own, Diana is venerated as She should be: The High-Priestess of all who work in witchcraft. Invoke Diana to help you do your Magicks, and to aid your power in Wicca to grow.

Pan is the complete focus of the forces of male fertility, and the complementary force to Diana. Fertility was very important to the people of old, because it represented to them, quite literally survival. Hence, the god of fertility and Diana, the Mother of All Living are the most important forces in the Universe, according to basic Wicca. Since the beginning of time the Great Goddess has appeared in Man's art and story, but the Horned God is nearly as old. Drawings in caves tell us of his early existance, and the Celts worshipped him as Cernnunos, the stag-god. In all instances, his physical prowess and intense male energies should be remembered.

Diana and Pan are of the greatest importance. Their powers symbolize the basic yearnings and desires of Humanking. This is, after all, what Witchcraft is all about, to call up the basic power in your mind and turn your desires into reality--to better your conditions, or those of your kin.

Now we come to a point that is very tough to many people. The horned god quite often represents Evil to them. Undoubtedly this is due to fear of a "devil" that has been drummed into them since Childhood. We hope you will remember from the first lesson that the identification of the Horned God with the Christian Devil is false and untrue. The power represented by the Hored God is positive and beautiful. If anyone tries to trap you into identifying the Horned God with Satan, try to explain his true significance. Go back to Lessons One and Four for the information printed there on the mistaken identification of the Christian Devil with the Horned God of the Wicca.

We now come to another subject of real importance. There are forces of varying strength in the Universe. The key to a successful ceremonie

210

is to use the right amount of power, no more and no less. It is best
not to call up a more powerful force than you need, lest the force over-
whelm you. There will be times when you will not need to call on a god-
force to accomplish your ends. There are many lesser forces (called
gods, angels, devas, sprites, fairies, elementals, and so on) that you can
call on for aid in your work. As a matter of fact, many of the so-called
'demons' of the ancient world were once the patron gods of tribes that
were in conflict with the Roman, Greek, or Hebrew nation-states. There
is a small book called the GOETIA (available from most Occult shops),
that contains methods for calling up about 72 of these little beasties.
Their powers and attributes are also listed in the GOETTIA, and many of
the spirits ahve very good and ehlpful qualities, stemming from their
days as _tulares_, or patron-gods. We believe you will find this book
very interesting. It has banishing as well as evoking spells in it,
which you should bear in mind, since all powers have thier destructive
as well as their helpful aspects, and this _is_ a book of Christian and
Judaic demonology.

You must do all types of work. Do not limit yourself. This is so
important that we feel we must constantly repeat it. Do not imbalance
your mind by working only with one certain aspect and no others.

      Use all the planetary powers.

      Practice invocation as well as evocation.

      Learn to control and perform all types of work. The mind is the
basic foundation for all work. Do not let some childish fears or
imaginary mosters prevent you from exerting your true will and taking
command of the Universe.

      Begin reading and studying, if you haven't already. We also recommend
that you set aside a place in your Book of Shadows for the attributes of
the various gods. Even though the amount you write may be brief, the
amount of information you carry in your mind will be greater, and will last
forever.

      We cannot encourage too strongly that you keep a record of all you
do, where magical works are concerned. The entrance requirements for
many Magickal organizations require such records.

* *

PHASES AND TIMES FOR WORKING SPELLS

As we have stated, the two greatest divisions are the two major phases
of the moon; waxing and waning. Work of a beneficial nature, as well
as work where one is charging an amulet or talisman with Power is usually
done when the Moon is waxing to Full. The most power is available between
the First and Second Quarters, when the Moon is rapidly growing Full.
When the Moon is waning to darkness, the time is perfect for works of a
more negative sort. Necromancy, spells to get rid of things, from a bad
habit to some extra inches, and other works of destructive nature are
done in this time. The dark of the Moon is the most ominous time of all;
reserved for operations of Death and Destruction. We do not recommend
that you do any operations at this time, and always remember that under
the Law of the Threefold Return, any magickal operation you do will have
three times the effect on you that it does on its victim.

The very fact of doing the spell in the Day or the Night has an
effect on it's form. Generally spells for good (apollonian, solar,
patriarchal) purposes are done during the day, preferably before Noon so
that the Sun is still waxing in power and there remain some hours of
daylight to increase the power generated.

Spells during the Dark Hours are for matters of a lunar, female/
feminist/matriarchal, and Dianic or Dionesian nature. These inlcude
but are not limited to enchantments, or influencing the will or another
(remember that Threefold Return!). These are frequently planned to
begin at moonrise, or even earlier, so that there will be some hours of
darkness following to enable the Power begun to blossom.

When at all possible, the seasons of the earth should be taken intp
consideration. This, of course, would be cumbersome for every spell,
but you will find that it helps you not to work against such strong
currents. If you are planning on owrking the great Solar Tides, waxing
moon spells would be done between the Winter Solstice and the Summer
Solstice, when the Sun is waxing, and waning spells would be done between
Midsummer and Yule, when the power of the Sun is shrinking and the days are
growing shorter. There are also the Eight Tides of the Year, which begin
at each of the Cross-quarter Days and change polarity at the Sabbats, but
this is not the place to discuss them. The degree and amount of the
power of the Sun at the various points in the whell of the year thus help
to set up the conditions by which more detailed and important work can

be accomplished.

The signs of the Zodiac play an important role in the working of various spells. Again, let me state that a spell or charm can be done anytime; it is just that sometimes have proven themselves more favorable than others.

* *

PLANETARY HOURS

In establishing what hours are ruled by the various planets proceed in the following manner: Find the hours of sunrise and sunset for the day in question. Midway between these is either the middle of the night or the middle of the day. Please note that this very seldom falls at either 12 noon or 12 midnight. Place this median time between the sixth and seventh hours of either chart given below, and figure your hours from there.

The powers of each of these heavenly boides are very numerous and complex, but briefly they are as follows:

213

HOUR	SUNDAY	MONDAY	TUESDAY	WEDNESDAY	THURSDAY	FRIDAY	SATURI
SUNRISE							
1	Sun	Moon	Mars	Mercury	Jupiter	Venus	Saturr
2	Venus	Saturn	Sun	Moon	Mars	Mercury	Jupite
3	Mercury	Jupiter	Venus	Saturn	Sun	Moon	Mars
4	Moon	Mars	Mercury	Jupiter	Venus	Saturn	Sun
5	Saturn	Sun	Moon	Mars	Mercury	Jupiter	Venus
6	Jupiter	Venus	Saturn	Sun	Moon	Mars	Mercu
7	Mars	Mercury	Jupiter	Venus	Saturn	Sun	Moon
8	Sun	Moon	Mars	Mercury	Jupiter	Venus	Saturr
9	Venus	Saturn	Sun	Moon	Mars	Mercury	Jupit
10	Mercury	Jupiter	Venus	Saturn	Sun	Moon	Mars
11	Moon	Mars	Mercury	Jupiter	Venus	Saturn	Sun
12	Saturn	Sun	Moon	Mars	Mercury	Jupiter	Venus
SUNSET							
1	Jupiter	Venus	Saturn	Sun	Moon	Mars	Mercu
2	Mars	Mercury	Jupiter	Venus	Saturn	Sun	Moon
3	Sun	Moon	Mars	Mercury	Jupiter	Venus	Satur
4	Venus	Saturn	Sun	Moon	Mars	Mercury	Jupit
5	Mercury	Jupiter	Venus	Saturn	Sun	Moon	Mars
6	Moon	Mars	Mercury	Jupiter	Venus	Saturn	Sun
7	Saturn	Sun	Moon	Mars	Mercury	Jupiter	Venus
8	Jupiter	Venus	Saturn	Sun	Moon	Mars	Mercu
9	Mars	Mercury	Jupiter	Venus	Saturn	Sun	Moon
10	Sun	Moon	Mars	Mercury	Jupiter	Venus	Satur
11	Venus	Saturn	Sun	Moon	Mars	Mercury	Jupit
12	Mercury	Jupiter	Venus	Saturn	Sun	Moon	Mars

214

MOON

Rules - Monday, Sign of Cancer
Trees - Willow
Herb - Chynostates
Daemonic Name - Lugh
Angelic Names - Gabriel, Bilet, Missaln, Abuzohn

Sigil - Gabriel   Shedbarshenoth Schartathen

Metal - Silver   Spirit - Phul
Colour - Silver
Operations - True heart, Astral travel, Safe journey
Stone - Pearl, Crystal, Spinel, Rose Quartz
Perfume - Camphor, Frankencense

37	78	29	70	21	62	13	54	5
6	38	79	30	71	22	63	14	46
47	7	39	80	31	72	23	55	15
16	48	8	40	81	32	64	24	56
57	17	49	9	41	73	33	65	25
26	58	18	30	1	42	74	34	66
67	27	59	10	51	2	43	75	35
36	68	19	60	11	52	3	44	76
77	28	69	20	61	12	53	4	45

Inscription - Hasmoda

9	Number of the planet	Hod
81	Number of the squares	Elim
369	Sum of a row	Hasmodai
3321	Number of planet multiplied by sum of row	Shedbanshenoth Schartathan
1312	Sum of perimeter	

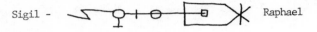

MERCURY

Rules - Wednesday, Sign of Gemini and Virgo

Trees - Hazel

Herb - Cinquefoil, Palm

Daemonic Name - Astaroth

Angelic Names - Raphael, Miel, Seraphiel, Tapthartharoth

Sigil -   Raphael

Metal - Quicksilver

Colour - Purple

Spirit - Ophiel   Astaphoi

Operations - Control of familiar, Success in commerce and business, Learn future
Influence

Stone - Amethyst, Lodestone, Agate

Perfume - Cloves, Cunquefoil

8	58	59	5	4	62	63	1
49	15	14	52	53	11	10	56
41	23	22	44	45	19	18	48
32	34	35	29	28	38	39	25
40	26	27	37	36	30	31	33
17	47	46	20	21	43	42	24
9	55	54	12	13	51	50	16
64	2	3	61	60	6	7	57

Inscription - Tiriel

8	Number of the planet	Asbogg
64	Number of squares	Din
260	Sum of a row	Tiriel
2080	Number of planets multiplied by sum of row	Tapthartharoth
910	Sum of perimeter	

216

♀

VENUS

Rules - Friday, Sign of Libra and Taurus
Trees - Myrtle
Herb - Verbena, Vervain, Fennel, Rose
Daemonic Name - Bechard
Angelic Names - Anael, Rachiel, Sachiel, Bne Seraphin

Sigil -   Anael

Metal - Copper
Colour - Green, Emerald
Spirit - Hagiel Ovraios
Operations - Works of lore or favour, Acquire beauty, To foster friendship,
          To ensure pleasure
Stones - Emerald, Amethyst, Carbuncle, Pearl
Perfume - Musk, Ambergris, Lignum Aloes, Sandalwood, Benzoin

22	47	16	41	10	35	4
5	23	48	17	42	11	29
30	6	24	49	18	36	12
13	31	7	25	43	19	37
38	14	32	1	26	44	20
21	39	8	33	2	27	45
46	15	40	9	34	3	28

Inscription - Kedemel

7	Number of Planet	Aha
49	Number of squares	Hagiel
175	Sum of a row	Kedemel
1225	Number of planets multiplied by sum of row	Bina Seraphin
600	Sum of a perimeter	

SUN

Rules - Sunday, Sign of Leo
Tree - Laurel
Herb - Poliginis
Daemonic Name - Surget
Angelic Names - Michael, Dardael, Hurtepul, Hachiel

Sigil -   Michael

Metal - Gold
Colour - Gold, Yellow
Spirit - Och (He)   Adonai
Operations - Construction Altar Cloth, Success and honour, Create harmony, Acquire
          money, Obtain patronage, Create Peace, Recover lost property.
Stones - Jacinth, Sunstone, Sardony
Perfumes - Cloves, Frankincense, Musk

6	32	3	34	35	1
7	11	27	28	8	30
24	14	16	15	23	19
13	20	22	21	17	18
25	29	10	9	26	12
36	5	33	4	2	31

Inscription - Elohem

6	Number of Planet	Vau
36	Number of squares	He
111	Sum of row	Eloh
666	Number of planet multiplied by sum of a row	Hachiel
370	Sum of a perimeter	

218

MARS

Rules - Tuesday, Sign of Scorpio and Aries
Tree - Cedar
Herb - Plantain
Deamonic Name - Flimost
Angelic Name - Samael, Satael, Amebiel, Graphiel

Sigil -   Samael

Metal - Iron
Colour - Red
Spirit - Phaleg   Saba
Operations - Making Pentacles when the Moon is in Virgo, War, Causing discord,
             Disrupting friendships
Stones - Ruby, Emerald, Jasper, Topaz
Perfume - Euphorbim, Bdellium, Rootsy Hellbore

11	25	7	20	3
4	12	25	8	16
17	5	13	21	9
10	18	1	14	22
23	6	19	2	15

Inscription - Adhi

5	Number of the planet	He
25	Number of the squares	Phaleg
65	Sum of a row	Adonai
325	Number of planet multiplied by sum of row	Graphiel
208	Sum of perimeter	

4

JUPITER

Rules - Thursday, Sign of Sagitarius and Pisces
Tree - Pine
Herb - Henbane
Daemonic Name - Silcharde
Angelic Names - Sachiel, Cassiel, Asasiel, Johphiel

Sigil -   K   Sachiel

Metal - Tin
Colour - Azure
Spirit - Bethor   Eioi
Operations - Construct Sword, Obtain health, Obtain power, Obtain friendship
Stones - Sapphire, Lapis Lazuli, Cornelian, Diamond, Pearl, Moonstone
Perfume - Lignum Aloes, Storax

4	14	15	1
9	7	6	12
5	11	10	8
16	2	3	13

Inscription - El Ab

4	Number of the planet	Aba
16	Number of the squares	Sachiel
34	Sum of a row	El Ab
136	Number of planet multiplied by sum of row	Johphiel
102	Sum of perimeter	

♄

SATURN

Rules - Saturday, Sign of Aquarius and Capricorn
Tree - Oak
Herb - Assodilius
Daemonic Name - Nabam
Angelic Names - Cassiel, Machatan, Uriel, Agiel

Sigil - ⟨𝓃⟩   Cassiel

Metal - Lead
Colour - Black
Spirit - Aratron   ILde Baoth
Operations - Constructing Pentacles and Athames, Works of Power, Astral knowledge, Esoteric Knowledge
Stones - Turquoise or Garnet
Perfume - Henbane and Mandrake, Poppy and Myrrh

4	9	2
3	5	7
8	1	6

Inscription - Jehova

3	Number of the planet	Ab
9	Number of squares	Hod
15	Sum of a row, column or diagonal	Jah
45	Number of planet multiplied by sum of row	Agiel
40	Sum of perimeter	

GLOSSARY

Bard--An ancient teacher who taught by the use of poems and
      song.

Bardien--Welsh plural for Bards.

Cantref--Similar to tribal lands or country.

Craft--Witchcraft or Wicca craft referring to CRAFT of the
      Wise Ones.

Cymmry--The Welsh name for the Welsh people.

Dawnsio--To dance

(y) dehev--The South

(y) Dewianath Cymmry--Welsh Paganism (Witchcraft) pre-dating
                      Christianity.

Drwy y nos, Canu--"To sing through the night."

(y) dwyrain--The East

Dynion Mwyn (Dynyn Myn)--Gentle Folk

(y) gogledd--The North

(y) grllewin--The West

Gwiddon (Gwillion)--Witch Priest/ess

Gwlad yr Hav--Summerland (Astral Plane)

Io EvoHe--"Hail to the (Great Spirit)"

Levez dew--Blessingupon (this)

Majorca--One of the Balaric Islands off the coast of Spain

Offieriade/ss--Priest or Priestess

Triads--Prose writings of three lines containing morals and
        guides to daily living.

Weir--Net placed across a small inlet to catch the fish as
        the tide goes out.

Wicca; Witch--Wise One; Priest or Priestess; Anglo-Saxon
            derived word.

Y Tylwyth Teg--Literally "The Fairy Folk;" also, "The
            Beautiful Family;" a clan of Priests and
            Priestesses who are members of the tribe of
            Dynion Mywn, "The Fair Family."